Keyworth 1
A Century of
Change

Keyworth & District Local History Society

1994

First published in 1994 by Keyworth & District Local History
Society
c/o Keyworth Library
Church Drive
Keyworth
Notts
NG12 5FF

Made and printed in Great Britain by The Local History Press,
3 Devonshire Promenade, Lenton, Nottingham NG7 2DS.

ISBN 0 9524602 0 3

Contents

Front cover by Peter Meade

Drawings on pages 8, 19, 66, 84, 85 and 89 by Haidee-Jo Summers

The map on page 2 and graph on page 99, orginally drawn for 'Keyworth — The Evolution of an East Midlands Village' by Bob Hammond in *Trent Geographer* No.15, 1994, are by Linda Dawes of the Department of International Studies, The Nottingham Trent University.

Foreword

'There was no labyrinth so intricate as the chaos of local law'
(H.H. Fowler, House of Commons 21 March 1893)

The bill introduced to the House of Commons by H.H.Fowler in March 1893 aimed to simplify local government. In his opening speech he pointed out that for local government purposes an inhabitant of a borough lived in a fourfold area viz., a borough, a parish, a union and a county. None of these was coterminous unless by accident with any of the others. In total, 28,343 authorities of a dozen different kinds could levy taxes in England and Wales.

Only a comprehensive bill could deal with such complexity. Its 71 clauses were grouped into five parts to deal with parish and district councils, boundaries, voting qualifications, accounts, borrowing powers, etc. The first and largest part of the bill was devoted to the creation of civil parish councils. Fowler recognized the parish as being 'the oldest aggregation in this country of men for the purpose of self government and local administration.' The popular description of the measure as being 'The Parish Council Bill' indicates the significance of the parish in the minds of the public and the Commons alike.

The second reading, delayed by consideration of Irish Home Rule, prompted intense discussion in which Fowler spoke no fewer than 800 times, and 619 amendments were dealt with. The bill became a political football kicked between Lords and Commons three times before the Prime Minister, Gladstone, in his very last speech to the House, reluctantly accepted the Lords' amendments and the bill was passed on 1 March 1894.

Unfortunately the wide powers granted to the parish councils were nullified by the imposition of severe spending restrictions so that they never achieved the importance in local administration envisaged by Fowler and his supporters. Nevertheless, for villages like Keyworth, the parish council is the first port of call on any matter concerning village life and has an important role in the development of social cohesion, the feeling of belonging to a community. At a time when local government is again under scrutiny it can only be a matter for regret that the most local of administrative units has been ignored.

This book marks the centenary of the creation of Keyworth's parish council; it does not pretend to be a definitive history, but sets out to describe some of the changes that have taken place during the past one hundred years which have affected the lives of people who have made Keyworth their home.

It has been compiled by members of the Keyworth and District Local History Society, the majority of whom have never before been involved in a similar task. They have depended upon the help and the memories of many people, including some whose families have lived in the village for generations. The authors of the chapters gratefully acknowledge this help. Inevitably not all of these contributions have found a place in this book. Indeed, the most difficult task faced by the authors has been the selection and arrangement of the information to fit the available space. The Society hopes that this, its first publication, will stimulate further interest in the history of the village and enhance our appreciation of its past.

Peter W. Roper
Chairman, Keyworth and District Local History Society.

Chapter 1

Keyworth in the 1890s

A hundred years ago, Keyworth's population of 800 was little more than a tenth of its present size. The built-up area of the village was largely confined to Town Street (now called Main Street), a cluster of buildings around the Parish Church, extending along Selby Lane to the Board School and windmill, and a few terraces along Nottingham Lane (now Nottingham Road) between Rose Hill and Debdale Lane (Fig.1). The parish was also smaller: until 1984, its northern boundary ran along Debdale Lane and Nicker Hill, but it now reaches the old railway line, taking in Plumtree Park and the British Geological Survey.

Size apart, the village also looked very different then. Lined with farms, Town Street's nickname of 'Cow Muck Alley' speaks for itself. Most of the other roads were untarred, with grass verges - more like Lings Lane today. Keyworth had no mains drainage or water supply, gas or electricity, lamp posts or telegraph poles. There was a windmill but no squash court, there were smoky chimneys but no petrol or diesel fumes, there was a blacksmith and wheelwright but no travel agent or bank. The Square's village pump, pinfold for stray animals and stockingers' workrooms have been replaced by a bus shelter, gyrating cars and shops.

A more detailed account of what the village looked like in the 1890s is contained in the Centenary Parish Guide, and this chapter will focus on people and jobs. It draws heavily on census data, particularly those for 1891. This is a fairly accurate, but not infallible source: for instance, the 1891 schedules list 781 people in the parish, but the summary gives a population of only 771.

One striking difference between then and now was the proportion of young and old people. In 1891 nearly half the population of Keyworth were under 20 and only one in ten was over 60, compared with a quarter and one in five today. These differences reflect the higher birth and death rates of a hundred years ago. Parents had more children and, although child mortality was high, each generation was larger than the one before. Couples reared an average of four surviving children who, therefore, outnumbered their parents two to one. Today's couples have, on average, less than two children. Of course these are only averages. Families of ten or more children were not uncommon, though the older ones had usually left home before the younger were born, so that they were not all sleeping under one roof. Nevertheless, some of the smaller cottages must have been very crowded, with several children shar-

1

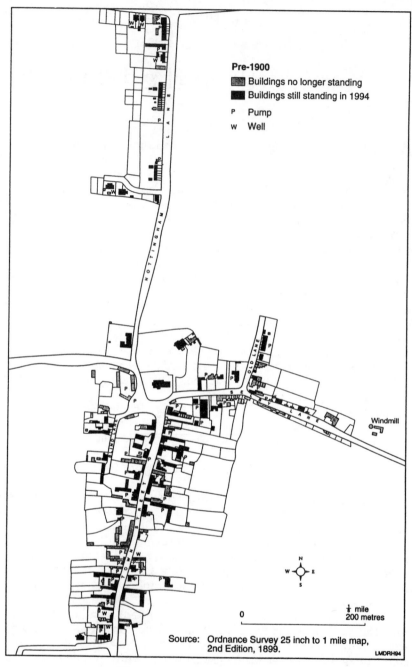

Windmill

Source: Ordnance Survey 25 inch to 1 mile map,
2nd Edition, 1899.

LMDRH94

Figure 1: Keyworth in the 1890s.

2

ing a bedroom or even one bed. Over a fifth of Keyworth households in 1891 contained seven or more members.

Life expectancy in rural England in the 1890s was only about 60, and much lower in towns: today it is 76. Numbers surviving beyond what we now call retiring age (there was no formal retirement age or pension then) were, therefore, few. Crowded living conditions, exacerbated in the case of consumption (TB) by drinking unpasteurised milk, facilitated the spread of infectious diseases, for many of which there was then no cure. Other than smallpox vaccination, there was no immunisation. Sanitary conditions were often rudimentary and there were no antibiotics. However, not all succumbed: our last living link with that final decade of Victorian Keyworth is Ethel Fenton, still going strong at 98 and the youngest but one of twelve children born to Thomas and Emma Disney. Apart from one who died as a child, all the offspring lived to be 79 or more, and one reached 100.

People's mobility in the 1890s was in many respects more restricted than today, both socially and geographically. Class barriers were harder to penetrate: most people seemed to accept the notion that 'God made them high and lowly and fashioned their estate'. Secondary education through Grammar and Public Schools, the gateway to the professions and most other high-status jobs, was almost entirely denied to working-class children until the 1902 Balfour Education Act.

Before the coming of the railway to Plumtree in 1880 most people in Keyworth walked everywhere, to school, to work, to the shops, to visit friends and relations. Not many could afford a bicycle let alone a horse. Carters operated a twice weekly carrier service to Nottingham but this was mainly for goods rather than passengers. People, therefore, rarely ventured more than a few miles from home and met few people from outside the village and its immediate neighbours. It is no surprise, therefore, that most people dwelt all their lives in the parish in which they were born. In Keyworth, 70% of the 1891 population were born in the parish and a further 14% in neighbouring Nottinghamshire villages south of the Trent. As a consequence, there were frequent liaisons between the same families. Nearly a third of Keyworth's population shared six family names: Pike, Simpson, Attewell, Disney, Eggleston and Hodgett. One should not, however, exaggerate the point: of the 140 married couples identified in the 1891 census, only 36% were both born in Keyworth, while in 22% of cases neither husband nor wife was born locally.

There were, in any case, two ways in which the population was highly mobile. Firstly, families frequently moved house within the village. Most houses were privately rented, so that a move did not usually involve the expense of selling and buying property; there were no Council Houses with waiting lists, and there was, in the 1890s, an oversupply of dwellings (12% were recorded as empty in the 1891 census). Moving was therefore easier than it is today, so as families grew and if finance permitted, they would move to larger or more convenient premises, though still within walking distance of wherever the breadwinner(s) worked. Between 1881 and 1891 a third

Framework Knitters' Workshop near corner of Main Street and Wysall Lane. Photographed 1993.

of households moved to at least one other address in Keyworth and many of those probably moved more than once.

Secondly, there was a huge outward migration of people from Keyworth in the last two decades of the nineteenth century. This was still a time when birth rates were far higher than death rates, so that natural increase alone should, at a conservative estimate, have produced an additional 150 people over those twenty years. Instead, the population decreased by 100 people between 1881 and 1891 and stagnated between 1891 and 1901. In other words, there was a shortfall over those two decades of some 250 people - between a third and a quarter of the 1881 population of just under 900. Coming as it did after a steady rise in population in line with natural increase over the previous 80 years at least, this deserves some explanation.

The main reason appears to have been the decline of Keyworth's staple nineteenth-century industry, framework knitting; and to a lesser degree of farming. Framework knitting had, since the invention of the stocking frame by William Lee of Calverton in the late sixteenth century, been a domestic industry not requiring any source of power other than human muscles. It was, therefore, well suited to villages within range of centres like Nottingham from which the industry was organised; lack of alternative employment meant that labour was cheaper than in towns. The knitting frames were either owned or rented by the men who worked them (few were worked by women). Cotton, wool and silk yarn was brought out, mostly from Nottingham, by

4

The Band of Hope outside the Board School, Selby Lane, c.1900

horse and cart (and train after 1880), to be worked up into strips of material. These were subsequently cut and sewn into stockings or gloves by seamstresses, who were often the wives and unmarried daughters of the frame operators. The finished products were then carried back to warehouses in Nottingham from where they would be sold all over Britain and abroad. Cotton hose (stockings) were the main product of the Nottingham trade but Keyworth, in mid-century at least, specialised in gloves. The 1861 census enumerator recorded that there were then twice as many glovers in the village as there were stockingers, with most of the gloves made from silk, presumably obtained from the only silk mill in the region, Lombe's Mill in Derby.

The procedure of 'putting out' work just described operated unchallenged throughout most of the eighteenth and nineteenth centuries with the East Midlands dominating the trade. After 1870, however, the scene began to change. British hosiers were being undercut in both overseas and home markets by German producers who introduced steam-powered machinery with much lower production costs. To meet the new competition, British manufacturers also began to mechanise, but to do this required access to cheap coal as well as larger production units. The writing was on the wall for domestic knitters in general and particularly for those in villages with no railway to bring in the coal. Older workers carried on for several decades but few young people joined them and the work force gradually aged until the industry died out. By the 1890s the process was well under way in Keyworth, with the proportion of knitters under 30 down from 62% in 1851 to 32% in 1891.

It might be thought that the new railway would have saved Keyworth's

5

Shaw's Farm, c.1900 with Mr Shaw and family in pony trap. (The house still stands on the corner of Main Street and Brookview Drive.)

industry from extinction, and indeed it did for over half a century. At least one powered factory, Pike and Gunn off Main Street, was established and continued in business until 1959, but once powered machinery replaced frames operated by hand and foot, the industry became much less labour-intensive and employed women almost exclusively. Young people, especially young men coming onto the labour market, had to look elsewhere for work.

Meanwhile farming was also undergoing a crisis. After 1870, cheap grain from the New World began to arrive in Britain, shortly to be followed by refrigerated meat and dairy produce. A long period of agricultural depression ensued which was only relieved by wartime blockades and the introduction of farm subsidies and import tariffs after the Second World War. Particularly hard hit were arable farmers on heavy soils like those of Keyworth, where production costs were high owing to the large teams of horses required to pull ploughs, and the frequent occasions when land was waterlogged and unworkable. Much arable land was put down to grass: in Keyworth the amount of cropland was halved and of pasture doubled between 1866 and 1896. Grassland generally requires less labour to maintain than crops, so again employment prospects were reduced. Although the railway brought Nottingham's expanding market in fresh milk and vegetables within range, alleviating the effects of depression, agriculture was in no position to absorb the surplus labour resulting from the decline in framework knitting.

There were few other occupations bringing money into the village. In 1861 there had been eleven cordwainers or shoe makers, suggesting a minor industry supplying more than Keyworth's needs. By 1891 this had fallen to four. The railway employed nine Keyworth men in 1891, and there were a number of sportsmen (mainly cricketers) who supplemented their meagre incomes with seasonal coaching contracts at public schools or by playing as professionals. The most distinguished was William Attewell, of whom there is more in chapter 6.

Most of the remaining occupants of Keyworth recirculated money within the village by providing services for its population. Ten shopkeepers are listed in Kelly's 1895 Directory, including three butchers, two bakers and two grocers, together with the blacksmith and wheelwright already mentioned, a miller, carpenter and watchmaker. Some of these small businesses probably employed several people. In addition, the 1891 census names one or more of the following: house painter, plumber, newsagent, chimney sweep, barber and carter. There were also two Inns (The Salutation and The Plough) both run by women in 1891 — Mary Davill and Elizabeth Neesham. The professions were represented by the doctor (Arthur Hare), the clergy (Henry Ling and Frederick Robinson, Anglican and Congregational respectively), the Police Constable (John Spence), and schoolteachers (Henry Neate, the Head and five others). There were no really rich residents in the village, so that openings in domestic service - the largest employer of young female labour nationwide - was limited. Even the Rector, probably the wealthiest, had only three servants, while the Rector of Plumtree kept seven.

Numbers in these service occupations depended largely on the declining number and prosperity of those engaged in industries bringing money into the village, and were, therefore, also in decline. In addition little building was taking place with a falling population, and activity in associated trades was scant: there had been nine bricklayers in 1861; in 1891 there were none.

Meanwhile, although the railway now made commuting to Nottingham possible, Keyworth people were slow to latch on. In 1890 only 34 season tickets were issued at Plumtree station, rising to 94 in 1900. Since most were three-monthly seasons, they represented respectively only some 9 and 24 people travelling daily to work from Plumtree station. Most of those probably did not come from Keyworth, which was further from the station than Plumtree, Normanton or newly developed Plumtree Park, then in Normanton parish.

It seems that most people looking for jobs outside Keyworth preferred to live near their work and left the village. Many young women must have gone into service in large town and country houses, while young men and women, either individually or with their whole family, moved to be near city factories, shops and offices, which generally offered higher wages than could be had in the village. Large numbers, therefore joined the exodus to towns which had depleted most rural settlements throughout the nineteenth century but to which industrial villages like Keyworth were an exception until their industries began to falter. That it was young adults who made up most of the exodus is attested by the fact that the age group 15-29 in 1891 constituted only 21% of Keyworth's population against a national average of 27%.

Keyworth in the 1890s was in a state of transition. The old order was changing and adjustment must have been painful for many. Both framework knitting and farm labouring were among the poorest-paid jobs for men in the country, and as their industries declined the weakly unionised workers had to accept still lower pay, face unemployment or seek better prospects away from family and friends. These rather bleak circumstances were, however, alleviated for some by their having more than one job. For instance Thomas Disney, Ethel Fenton's father, was a framework knitter but supplemented his income as school caretaker, while Peter Pike Attewell combined being a framework knitter and village postman. In addition, the allotments on the corner of Selby Lane and Willow Brook enabled many to grow their own vegetables, while there were a number of tenants or owners of smallholdings for whom the land provided their main but probably not their sole occupation. There were also the part-time professional sportsmen already mentioned.

Meanwhile the beginning of a new era was slowly dawning as the first commuters from Keyworth walked to Plumtree station to board trains to work. The trickle gathered momentum during the First World War, continued to grow as buses supplanted the railway in the 1920s, and turned into a flood with the rapid development of the village as a dormitory for Nottingham in the 1960s with the car now the main mode of travel.

Commuting continues unabated but the growth of the village has, for the time being at least, come to an end. Indeed, population has declined since the boundary extension in 1984 (see Chapter 12), as young families who settled here two or three decades ago have aged and their children have left home. In that respect at least, if in little else, Keyworth of the 1990s resembles Keyworth of the 1890s.

The Salutation Inn and adjoining thatched cottage.

Chapter 2

Keyworth Parish Council

The concept of the parish is very ancient, being part of a traditional hierarchy of areas (with county and hundred) going back to the Norman Conquest and beyond. The ecclesiastical parish was the basic unit of the poor law system, and became the administrative unit for most local purposes. For example, surveyors of highways were appointed on a parochial basis from 1555 and petty constables from 1662.

The Act of 1834 transferred poor law administration to Unions (comprising a number of parishes), Keyworth becoming part of the Bingham Union. In 1862, the creation of highway districts was embarked upon. In Nottinghamshire, the Justices tried to make their boundaries coincide with those of the poor law unions.

Under the 1870 Education Act, parishes in rural areas were required to provide a school, working through an ad hoc School Board. Keyworth School Board operated a school until it was taken over by the County Council following the 1902 Act.

The Local Government Act of 1894 replaced the existing forms of local government with a new system of elected councils. The first meeting of the newly elected Keyworth Parish Council was held on 31 December 1894, when the Rev Frederick Robinson (minister of the Congregational Chapel) was elected the first Chairman.

The new council quickly used its authority to improve village life. The first meetings were concerned with the provision of garden allotments, and the status of the (still existing) allotments at the corner of Selby Lane and Willow Brook. Under the Enclosure Award of 1798, this plot of land has been reserved for the benefit of the poor of Keyworth, being divided into allotments in 1844.

In 1898 the Parish Council drew up its own code of eight bye-laws for the parish, of which four were concerned with water supply and sewage disposal. Water supply, drainage and sewerage can make for fascinating reading, and Keyworth certainly had its problems. In theory, Keyworth was well placed for water, since the gravel beds under the old village contain a number of good springs, but the demand exceeded the supply.

At the turn of the century, water was available only from the parish pump (in the Square) and from a number of wells in gardens. Legal proceedings had to be taken against at least two parishioners before use of water for unauthorised purposes ceased to be a problem. It proved necessary to have a lock so that access to the pump could be restricted in times of shortage. For example, for a period in 1898, due to water shortage in the village, the pump was unlocked only from 12 noon to 1.30 p.m. each day.

Drainage and sewerage schemes came in only gradually. New main drains for Nottingham Road were laid in 1900, and for Debdale Lane in 1913. When in 1937 Bingham R.D.C. proposed a drainage scheme for part of the parish, the Parish Council asked for the inclusion of the whole village, listing Main Street, Elm Avenue and Nicker Hill as particular black spots. Concern continued to be expressed until well after the Second World War.

In 1949 culverts on Lings Lane and Wolds Lane were a problem, and in May 1950 field tenants were asked to keep cattle away from the newly cleaned sewer dyke from Lings Lane to Fairham Brook. Also in 1949 the Sanitary Inspector was informed of the nuisance of the emptying of lavatory pans in Dale Road and Nottingham Lane. Although in 1954 a new sewerage scheme was proposed for Keyworth, Stanton and Normanton, in 1957 Bingham R.D.C. was still spreading sewage over open fields near houses. During 1957 and 1958 residents had to contend with a sea of mud as the new sewers were installed.

Water supply made more rapid progress and by the thirties the village pump was falling into disuse and disrepair.

Refuse collection was often a matter of concern to the Parish Council, although not a direct responsibility: the work was contracted out. A minute such as that of 9 May 1913: 'Resolved that Notices be posted in the village that pans and other refuse would be taken away on Thursday 29th inst.' appeared at intervals over many years.

In 1896, although the main roads in the village came under Bingham R.D.C., the Parish Council was able to let grazing rights on the verges of, for example, Lings Lane.

References to footpaths are frequent in early council minutes, the majority relating to field paths. Between 1896 and 1901 there were repeated complaints about the path to Wysall, particularly the condition of the footbridges. The path to Bunny was a continual source of discussion, not only about its maintenance but also its exact location and status as a right of way. Over the years, the council was concerned about other footpaths: to Plumtree Station (1896, 1900), alongside Bunny Lane (1929), to Narrow Lane (1919), to Stanton (1935) and from Elm Avenue to Ashley Road (1947).

Postal services also concerned the council, asking for a second daily delivery in the village, and a telegraph office (1898, 1909 and 1911). By 1925 the council was asking that the second delivery be extended to the outlying parts of the parish. In the 1930s the council asked for extra postboxes.

Buses had appeared by the 1920s. By 1924 the council was concerned about traffic problems, such as buses obstructing the Square. Two companies were asked not to run their buses simultaneously, to give the village a better service. Operators often did not keep to time and litter from the buses was swept out in the Square. Gradually council concern shifted to the provision of extra bus stops and better indication of destinations. In 1945 the council tried to obtain a bus to take children to West Bridgford Grammar School. By

Keyworth Parish Council, 1960. Back row: Herbert Mills, Ralph Tatham, Alwyn Middleton, Harry Henson, Colin Troughton, William Davill. Front row: Newman Armstrong, Peter Witcomb, Reg Easton, Fred Green, Norman Brettle (Clerk).

1950 there was a pressing need for improved services and more bus stops and shelters. From 1986–87 the council was concerned with the effects of deregulation, until services reverted to something like the original situation, though with a number of changes to routes.

Street lighting was first discussed (and rejected) in 1895. After several unsuccessful efforts, in 1929 the council was finally empowered to spend £70 on six street lamps. This was gradually increased to 14 lamps by 1936. After the war there was cautious expansion in response to increased needs. Until 1957 expenditure had to be approved by the Annual Parish Meeting. Provision was sparse and in 1960 the Annual Meeting was told that Keyworth was 20 years behind the times. That meeting decided to erect 21 sodium lights on Keyworth's main streets but this was challenged and another special meeting had to be called. Fortunately 23 sodium lamps were approved and loan arrangements to cover the cost made with the County Council. Street lighting ceased to be a Parish responsibility in 1974.

Housing, although a District responsibility, has always concerned the Parish Council. After the First World War, the parish supported the introduction of council housing with a deputation to Bingham R.D.C. housing committee, recommending up to twenty houses for Keyworth. In 1927 the

11

Parish Council protested at Bingham's proposal to sell the remainder of its building site and wrote to the Ministry of Health that there was still a housing need in the village.

The expansion of housing in the village really began with the building of more council houses in 1950. The estate was enlarged in the years to 1959 partly to house National Coal Board employees as the Cotgrave mine began to be developed from 1956. The Wimpey, Goulding and other estates were perhaps foreshadowed in 1958 when a parish councillor enquired about a proposal to build council houses on Nicker Hill. An interesting suggestion was made in 1959 for the proposed extension of Church Drive to be a 24 foot wide carriageway. Needless to say, the normal 18 foot road was felt to be quite adequate.

Wimpeys tried to buy the Charity Allotments in the autumn of 1960, and after much negotiation a strip was sold to them in March 1963, to allow the Fairway to open into Willow Brook. By 1972 Costain were building their estate which completed the allotted development area.

The First World War occupied the council's attention only marginally, with references to various war charities, the National Agricultural Committee and the Local Food Committee. Although the council met on the evening of 11 November 1918, there is no reference at all to the Armistice. An anti-Government attitude is perhaps indicated by the council's letters to the Prime Minister, in 1920 objecting to British intervention in Poland against Russia and in 1927 protesting against the sending of troops to China.

In 1935 the local press accused the council of neglecting its duty to the Silver Jubilee celebrations. This charge was denied in the minute of 15 May that year, which also attacked the attitude of the Parochial Church Council and of the local British Legion. This controversy continued for some time and may explain why the 1937 parish elections saw five councillors of very long standing rejected and only two former councillors retaining their seats, although a number of former councillors did not stand for re-election.

The Second World War made more impact on council affairs. To comply with black-out regulations, meetings had to be held in the British Legion building. Volunteer helpers were called for to deal with evacuees. Council representatives served on committees for National Savings, the Spitfire Fund, and waste paper; while active help was given with raising funds for the war blind, parcels for prisoners of war, and Tank Week.

In the 1950s Keyworth was still a small, quiet place. Development had occurred along Nicker Hill and Normanton Lane, but the major part of Plumtree Park was in Normanton parish and this continued to confuse village administration until 1978. The parish was not concerned with housing development until at least 1964, so that in the 1950s residents could hardly envisage the changes so soon to be made.

The search for a burial ground and for recreational land preoccupied the Parish Council greatly in the 1950s. In fact, the search for a recreation ground had started in 1946. At this time sports clubs rented the Rectory Field so this was the obvious site. The land was owned by the Church, as part of Queen

Anne's Bounty, vested in the local Rector. The Church was reluctant to sell and it was not until 1952 that the field of just over five acres became council property. By 1951 two acres of adjoining land had been bought from Mr Poole, specifically for a children's play area.

The subsequent history makes for interesting research. Not the least was an early problem with drainage. In 1954 the state of the field caused speculation that its waterlogged condition was due either to the infilling of the pond or to the overflowing of wells in the Rectory garden.

Funding was a problem from the start. Grants were obtained after lengthy negotiations for the initial purchase but the laying out of the various pitches and the maintenance of sheds and pavilions were the subject of much discussion. An annual Gymkhana had at one time provided some funds for sports activities, but by December 1954 it was suggested that a charge would have to be made on the rates and by 1963 this was being seriously considered. Even so, much of the work on the field had to be done by volunteers.

The Playing Field management committee was set up in 1957, a twenty-one year lease signed in 1958, legalised, and a trust deed signed in 1963. By 1964 the tennis courts had been provided and the bowling green started. The search for recreational facilities did not end here. In 1973, both the swimming pool and Platt Lane playing fields were conceived as joint projects with County and District. A Gorse Road play area was provided during the same period by the Parish Council but vandalism caused this to be short-lived. It was hoped that the provision of the Platt Lane playing fields would enable the Rectory Field to be used as parkland, but this is still in the future.

The Stonepits on Widmerpool Lane were assigned in the Parish award for the perpetual use of Keyworth parish. When their original purpose became obsolete, efforts were made to find a new use. Eventually the area was maintained as a nature reserve but the disappearance of the access road made this difficult. In 1988 the land was exchanged for the conservation area on Lings Lane, which won county-wide awards in 1988 and 1992.

In 1952 it was agreed that a Scout hut could be erected on the playing fields, but the exact site was the subject of protracted discussion and the hut was not erected until 1955.

A village hall had been wanted for many years and the Rectory Field was thought to be a suitable site. Even so, in 1952 Butlers Factory was suggested and in 1959 prefabricated building brochures were considered at a Parish Council meeting. At last, at the 1964 Annual Parish Meeting, residents demanded a village hall and the Council set up a Village Hall sub-committee. The foundation stone was laid in 1968 by Mrs Bloor, at that time the oldest resident.

The hall has been repeatedly updated to meet local needs. The Community Room became a twinkle in the council's eye in about 1984, when councillors were anxious to provide more comfortable accommodation for senior citizens then using the South Wolds Youth Club.

Of great concern in 1947 was the realisation that the Parish Church graveyard was nearly full. The search for land in this case was hampered by legal

13

Twinning Ceremony, 1977. Left to right: Henri Prévost (Chief Executive Feignies Administration), Derek Twiss (Clerk to Keyworth Parish Council), Colin Cawthorn (Chairman, Keyworth Parish Council), Jean Jarosz (Mayor of Feignies), ?, Bernard Coyne, ?, ?, ?.

and agricultural problems as well as by a natural reluctance of owners to sell. Sites were considered off Commercial Road, but in one case the land was of too high an agricultural quality and the other so near to a number of properties that it was unlikely that all the owners would give their permission under the 100 yards rule.

The Mill Field on Selby Lane was thought to be suitable, but eventually Barlows Paddock near the site of the Village Pond on Wysall Lane was chosen. Negotiations took so long that in 1953 only seven spaces were left in the Parish Churchyard. Even so the Wysall Lane site was not consecrated until September 1955, with the first interment in 1963. At this time out-of-parish burials cost twice as much as local ones, while registration of deaths had to be made at Bingham until 1957.

Population growth in the village brought its share of benefits and problems. Dr Rhind had retired in 1948 after 46 years in the village. In 1957 Dr Russell, his successor, reacted promptly to demands for better surgery facilities and a child welfare clinic in Keyworth to save mothers travelling to Plumtree.

School provision did not keep pace with the new estates. In 1948 there had been a complaint that there was a lack of discipline in the village school

Centenary Lounge, built 1993

and that better use could be made of pupils' last two years. Throughout the 1950s there were demands for better·classroom accommodation, better lavatories and more progress reports. A protest meeting in 1960 complained that children had to be taught in a lecture hall, although in 1957 there were plans to extend the school for 120 more pupils.

The Nottingham Road school was begun in 1962. Negotiations for land for South Wolds School started in July 1960 and it was built in 1964. Crossdale School was built in 1974. Until the provision of schools was reasonably adequate children were taken to Lutterell School in West Bridgford and, for a while, under a storm of protest, to Musters Road School.

Refuse collection, street cleaning and a lack of public telephones came under constant scrutiny from the Parish Council. Vandalism and policing, the promotion of local business, and environmental problems are all mentioned continually throughout the 100 years of the council. The Community Concern Committee started in 1974 as a result of the council's efforts to help the elderly during the power emergency.

Local Government re-organisation in 1974 emphasised the local importance of parish councils. In 1894 Keyworth had eleven councillors, in 1961 thirteen, and seventeen since the parish was extended to include parts of Normanton. The full council and its six committees each meet approximately monthly, so councillors now spend much more time on council (i.e. village) business than was necessary even forty years ago. Additionally, sub-committees are appointed as necessary to deal with particular, temporary aspects of council business.

In 1977, the village was twinned with the French town of Feignies, and each year the Parish Council and the independent twinning committee renew contacts with their counterparts in Feignies.

The Parish Council has laboured continuously for one hundred years. Its work is slowly but steadily pursued in the interests of the residents; examples appear in its care of its property, the ongoing refurbishment of the Village Hall and the play area and, in particular, the construction of the Centenary Lounge in 1993, which was officially opened by the Rt. Hon. Kenneth Clarke Q.C., M.P. on 10 June 1994. In the interests of the wider community it has sought to persuade District and County to maintain and improve roads and business areas. Successes include the improved appearance of The Square and The Parade and its awards in the Best Kept Village competitions of 1970 and 1990.

Chapter 3

The Churches and People

For a long time the religious landscape in Keyworth was unchanged. It was only in the 1960s, that great decade of social change, that there was a shift in religious allegiance and in the relations between the Churches.

In 1894 the Independent and Primitive Methodist Chapels had larger congregations than the Parish Church. There was no lord in Keyworth to uphold the Anglican Establishment, although the Parish Church was one of the largest landowners in the village. In 1878 there had been a bitter conflict between the Parish Church and the nonconformist chapels over the opening of the Board School on Selby Lane and relations remained sour for many years.

There were radical Protestant groups in Keyworth and groups connected with the Baptists. But these were small and it is difficult to find records which refer to them. At this time, Roman Catholics were limited to a few families who worshipped elsewhere.

Change was slow until the 1960s, although religion no longer dominated life as it did a century ago. Secular organisations like the League of Nations Union attracted the people of Keyworth. There was an increasing number of families in which the partners belonged to different denominations. It was a sign of increasing tolerance that such families could live in harmony with each other and their neighbours. But, even as late as 1955, there was religious disagreement over the new burial ground on Wysall Lane. The Bishop of Southwell was asked to bless the new cemetery, but the Congregational Minister objected because he felt that the new cemetery should be non-denominational.

In the 1960s new housing estates led to an influx of people from outside and Keyworth's population more than doubled (see Chapter 12). The existing churches recruited new members. For the first time a Catholic community was established, which was helped by the establishment of Mary Ward College in 1968. But many of the newcomers had no religious affiliation.

One effect of the decline in religious practice was to draw the Churches closer together. When Mary Ward College closed in 1977 the Anglican, United Reformed and Methodist Churches offered their premises for Catholic services. This would never have happened in an earlier era.

The Youth Concert with Sister Beuno and Father Gilroy, 1970–1990.

The Roman Catholic Church in Keyworth

For many years there were few Catholic families in Keyworth. Before the Second World War Henry Passam and his family of a boy and a girl lived in Keyworth, but they have since left the village. Pat Boyle lived in Keyworth until his death in 1993. The nearest Roman Catholic Church was in West Bridgford.

In the 1950s and 1960s young families began to move into Keyworth. The opening of Cotgrave Pit and the building of the Council Estate led to families moving from the North-East of England. For others, Keyworth was a pleasant village to start a new home, with easy access to Nottingham. Some of these families were Roman Catholic and many of them still live in Keyworth. In 1961 Fr Buckley from West Bridgford began to say Mass in the British Legion. He used to carry the vestments in an old suitcase which he had acquired while serving as an army chaplain during the war. The suitcase is now in the Roman Catholic Church on Willow Brook. Sometimes a priest came from St Hugh's, Tollerton, which was a seminary for preparing boys for the priesthood. In 1964 Keyworth became part of the parish of Radcliffe-on-Trent where Fr Wilson was the Parish Priest. By this time services took place in the Anglican Church Hall on Selby Lane.

The opening of Mary Ward College in 1968 increased the number of Roman Catholics because many of the students were Irish. Some lived with families in Keyworth and some of the former students settled in the village and are members of the Roman Catholic Community. The chapel of Mary Ward College was used for services but in 1977 the College closed and the buildings, including the chapel, were sold to the British Geological Survey.

All the Churches in Keyworth offered to share their premises with the Roman Catholic Church. The Methodist Church was chosen because it had more seating accommodation than the Anglican or United Reformed Churches. In 1985 the new Roman Catholic Church on Willow Brook was completed. During these years the Catholic priest was Fr John Gilroy, who was formerly a missionary in Africa. He spent much of his time in Keyworth and was highly regarded by the other Churches in Keyworth. He was assisted in his work by Sister Beuno, a Dominican nun, who lives in Keyworth. He also received much support from the Union of Catholic Mothers. In 1990 Fr Gilroy was succeeded by Fr Stephen Foster. The present Parish Priest is Fr John Abbott.

The United Reformed Church

The United Reformed Church used to be known as the Congregational Church and before that as the Independent Chapel. The first Independent Chapel in Keyworth was built in 1768 and this made the Independents the oldest religious group in Keyworth after the Church of England. It was a well-established community in 1894. The Pastor lived in the Manse which is now the Headquarters of the British Legion. The Church owned land where Nottingham Road Junior School and the Council Estate are now established. The Congregation included men of substance like Randolph Kemp Hodgett, a local framework knitter and businessman who played an important role in the Church until his death in 1944.

Many societies flourished at the Church. Miss Henrietta Hodgett helped

Pastor and Mrs Birkitt 1933–1947

to organise the Sunday School in the 1890s. A popular event was the tea held in the field behind the Congregational Church. The Women's Guild, which was founded in the 1920s, raised funds for the Missions and for improvements at the Church as well as giving donations to the League of Nations Union for Czech children fleeing from German occupation. In spite of these activities, Congregationalists and Methodists felt they were second class citizens compared with members of the Anglican Church. This explains why, politically, the Congregationalists tended to support the Liberal Party and the Methodists the Labour Party.

The Church numbered some strong personalities in its ministers. The Rev F. Robinson was the first Chairman of the Parish Council. He was also an assistant teacher at the Board School in Selby Lane which had been founded in opposition to the Anglican School. Later, in 1927, he became a member of the League of Nations Union.

Pastor Birkitt was at Keyworth from 1933 to 1947. He was a railwayman before he entered the ministry. During the War he went out of his way to help evacuees from Sheffield and Great Yarmouth who were sent to Keyworth. He found them places with families and personally visited them to see that they were being looked after. He was a generous man who gave his own possessions to the needy. A strong supporter of the temperance movement, his sermons on Temperance Sundays were focused on the evils of alcohol. He was regarded as a man of God.

His successor was a student-pastor from the Patten College at Tollerton Hall, Arthur Nagle. Later Arthur Nagle became a full time pastor and he still visits Keyworth. He was succeeded in 1949 by Rev F.G.H. Sleath, who stayed until 1954. In that year the Rev R.C. Plowright became Pastor. He had a daughter who was a missionary in India and much of the fund raising carried out by the Women's Guild was sent to India. The Boys' Brigade branch was founded by him and he took a keen interest in the Youth Club. He encouraged closer ties with the Methodists. He visited people when he was needed and some families were grateful to him because of his care for people who did not belong to the Congregational Church. The role played by the wives of the Pastors in helping and supporting the Church must not be forgotten.

In 1961 the members and deacons of the Church invited Miss June Davis to become Pastor. In this way the Church recognised the increasing role played by women in society and proved that it could adapt to change.

The Anglican Church

From 1878 to 1927 the Rector of Keyworth was Rev Henry Pratt Ling. He inherited a bitter conflict over the Board School, but he seems to have been a thoughtful and considerate man. Some say that Lings Lane was named after him and it is said that he would visit anyone — no matter what denomination they belonged to. He was more conciliatory than his predecessor. When,

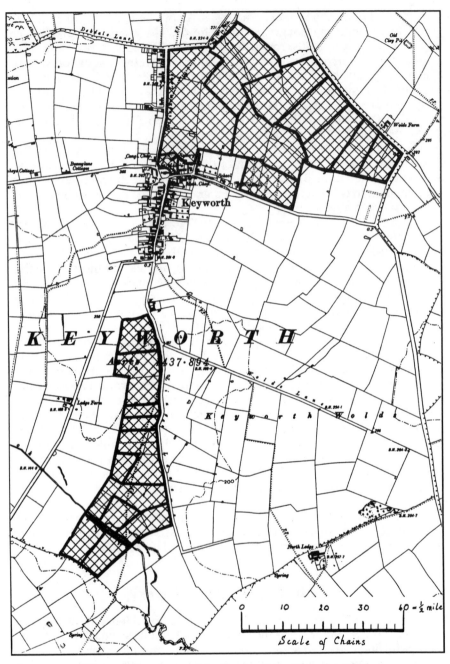

Figure 2: Land owned by the Anglican Church c.1914.

22

The Church in the pre-car era.

in 1894, the Board School needed improvements, the Rector offered the Church school as accommodation for the infants. The offer was declined. In the 1920s he became a member of the League of Nations Union, which had a lively branch in Keyworth. At the Parochial Church Council, he urged the laity to play a role in Church affairs. In many ways he was ahead of his time. But his congregation was less numerous than the Congregational and Methodist Churches. In 1909 only 14 attended the service on Palm Sunday and the numbers rose to 50 on Easter Sunday. His farewell sermon in 1927 was attended by 50 people.

He lived in the Rectory — a house with six bedrooms built in 1869. As a result of the Enclosure Act of 1798, the Church owned a farm of 283 acres at Normanton-on-the-Wolds, as well as 230 acres in Keyworth. The Keyworth land included what is now the Wimpey Estate and land between Lings Lane and the Wysall Road (Figure 2). Much of the land was sold in 1918 and was purchased by tenants who farmed the land. These included James Oldham and William Webster. Further sales were made in 1930. The money was not invested wisely and the finances of the Church were not healthy. In 1921 the Church wall along Selby Lane collapsed and a house to house collection was organised to pay for its repair.

On the Rector's retirement in 1927, the Rev Percy Rushmer became the priest in residence. The former rector still retained the living. In this sense the new minister was on probation. He was 'high church' and described himself as 'a priest of the Catholic Church'. He was, personally, popular, but towards the end of 1928 his attendance in the parish became erratic. The Preachers' book records that there were no weekday services during Advent because the Rector was indisposed. He last said mass on 15 September 1929 and failed to attend a parochial church council meeting on 17 October. Relations between the Minister and the Parochial Church Council became strained. The P.C.C. wrote to the Bishop of Southwell requesting a new minister and the Bishop was sympathetic to the request.

The Rev Henry Ling was still the patron and he transferred the living to the Bishop, who then transferred it to the Rev Basil Brooker. He became both Rector and Patron. He was a hard-working minister who had previously served at Mansfield Woodhouse and Calverton. He took four services on Sunday — three at Keyworth and one at Stanton-on-the-Wolds. He described himself as a minister of 'the Established Church', unlike his predecessor. One innovation was a special service for golfers. This may reflect the changes in Keyworth society as much as his own enthusiasm. There was a rise in the numbers attending the Anglican Church. In 1938, 96 were present on Easter Sunday and 48 on Whit Sunday.

Although the increased congregation and the sale of Church land put the parish finances on a sound basis, the Rector himself seems to have been pressed for money. In 1936 his elder son was a boarder at Worksop College where the fees were £70 p.a. In a letter the Headmaster wrote to the Rector stating that the younger boy could qualify for a smaller fee if he won a scholarship or exhibition.

Increased attendances at the Parish Church may have been partly explained by the threat of war and attendances remained high during the War. A 'National Day of Prayer' was held on Saturday 25 May 1940, just before Dunkirk, when 42 were present. One of the Rector's sons was killed during the War. Rev Brooker remained Rector until 1949 when he resigned. He died the following year.

The Parochial Church Council asked for a family man to be appointed as the new Rector and the Rev George Fry was selected. He was concerned with the dignity of the services and care of the fabric and surroundings of the Parish Church. New vestments and hymnbooks were purchased and special attention was paid to the choir led by Mr A. Disney, who was to become an ordained minister. The Church wall was repaired by Mr Middleton and a motor mower was purchased to keep the churchyard tidy. The Rev Fry was a methodical man and he gave an annual report of progress to the Parochial Church Council. These reports indicate how the finances of the parish were improving, but he was concerned about the lack of interest shown by young people in religion. To remedy this the Rector began to visit the new Council Estate.

The old rectory was sold and, in 1954, part of the old glebe was sold to the Parish Council on condition there were no organised games on a Sunday. This land today forms part of the Recreation Ground.

The Rev Fry was highly regarded in the diocese and was made an Honorary Canon of Southwell Minster in 1958. But in 1960 he became ill and died shortly afterwards. He was succeeded by the Rev J. Gibson, who was a Vicar at Netherfield. Numbered amongst the members of the Parochial Church Council in 1961 was Alan Armstrong, in 1994 a long-serving Churchwarden, and his membership could mark the point where history ends and the modern age begins.

The Methodist Church

Keyworth Methodist Church was founded in 1818 as part of the Primitive Methodist movement then establishing itself in the Midlands. Led by William Pike and his family, the Society, as early Methodist groups were known, grew considerably and by the 1890s was an important part of village life. The present church was built in 1881 and the church hall in 1886, although there have been later extensions. The 1891 schedules record 73 members, with a Sunday School totalling 166 children, with 21 teachers. It was said that '300 persons attended the chief services'; presumably this number includes all who attended from time to time.

It is clear from old registers that this church appealed especially to the large number of framework knitters in the village who, no doubt, felt themselves estranged from the other churches. The Primitive Methodist Chapel became for many a centre of their whole social existence. Sundays were busy days, especially for the children: two sessions of Sunday School, one in the morning and one in the afternoon, followed by two preaching services at 2.30 p.m. and 6.00 p.m. This regime lasted well into the twentieth century — it forms part of the childhood memories of many elderly people today. In addition there were extra services during the week and meetings of the small groups traditionally known in Methodism as classes. Music was provided by a small orchestra.

The church was also active in educational and purely social activities. Reading and writing were taught, in weeknight classes as well as on Sundays. Social gatherings took place from time to time: there were prize-givings and outings for the children.

There has never been a Methodist minister resident in Keyworth and in pastoral charge of the church, so the Methodist community had to be self-reliant. Services were conducted by the ministers and local preachers of the Nottingham No. 4 circuit, of which Keyworth was a part. Most of these people came from West Bridgford or the City, though in 1891 there was one, a Mr J. Simpson, in Keyworth, and a Mr S. Wright listed as a 'helper' (who may on occasion have conducted worship). Mr Wright later became a full local preacher; he also, together with three members of the Pike family, led an evangelical group who led worship in other chapels, particularly at Bunny (where there is now no Methodist Church). By the 1890s two Methodists were active in parish affairs, especially in connection with the school board

Methodist Church Outing c.1930.
Back Row: George Lacey, Deborah Tomlinson, Winnie Hodgett, Mrs
C.Tomlinson, Claude Tomlinson.
Middle Row: Nellie Lacey, ?Mrs Orange, Miss Sigger.
Front Row: Kathleen Terzza, Gertrude Lacey, Mary Allen, Mrs Cooper, Maria
Tomlinson.
In Front: Rhoda Foster (née Murden).

and the new Parish Council. They campaigned against drinking and other social problems common in the circles in which they moved.

Relations with other churches varied. With the Congregational Church (now U.R.C.) they were good: the Congregational minister was always welcome in the Methodist Chapel. Occasionally the two congregations joined for worship, usually on special Sundays. After the controversy over the building of a Board School in the 1870s the two groups worked together in local affairs. There was, however, much animosity against the Parish Church, for both theological and social reasons. The Anglicans were absent from the opening celebrations for the Chapel in 1881: the Rector of Widmerpool wished to be present but his Bishop expressly forbade him to attend. That such things would now be unheard of is an indication of the extent of change in religious attitudes during the last hundred years.

The 1890s were in many respects a high point in the history of Keyworth Methodist Church. At that time a high proportion of the population went to church more or less regularly and this church was a flourishing one. The twentieth century has been a time of decline in church-going, though at first this was not obvious. The Keyworth Methodists continued to develop their church life. Music in worship was enhanced with the installation of a pipe organ in 1905; in 1908 the Primitive Methodist Church was celebrating its centenary all over the country and celebrations took place in Keyworth. The well known photograph of Keyworth Methodist Choir which appears in several publications on local history was taken on this occasion. The church formed a Young People's Committee in 1912 which busied itself over a number of years in arranging special services and activities for the youth of the church. In 1928 the centenary of the original chapel was celebrated and the jubilee of the present church in 1931: at this the village joked about having a centenary before the 50th anniversary.

Nineteenth-century Methodism had become noted for dividing into several different denominations, often over matters which may seem trivial to us today. But the twentieth century saw a reversal of this tendency: in 1932 the three largest groups, which included an overwhelming majority of Methodist churches, united to form the present Methodist Church in Great Britain. The Keyworth church forms part of that national church; locally it forms part of the Nottingham South Circuit. This is how things were when after the Second World War Keyworth began to expand. Then a church which was, like other churches, gradually declining and reliant on an ageing congregation, was able to reach out to a new population with the result that today the membership is higher than it has ever been, and it is indeed at present one of the larger Methodist communities in South Nottinghamshire.

Conclusion

Since the 1960s the pace of change has slackened. The Churches have remained independent with their own premises and societies. The number of denominations has increased due to a revival locally of the Baptist Church. But there has been a change in attitude. There is a greater openness compared with earlier in the century and much of the suspicion which existed between the Churches has disappeared. The Keyworth Inter-Church Committee was set up to organise joint services and discussion groups. For many years a 'Silent Witness' has taken place on Good Friday when people from all Churches walk in silence from the Parade to the Square as a reminder of Christ's death on the cross. But this co-operation has stopped short of unity. Before the 'Sixties' the Churches supported their own charities and missionary societies. This has changed. Support is now given to non-denominational groups such as the Macedon Trust and relief agencies working in the Third World.

Chapter 4

The Changing Educational Scene

Education, like other aspects of Keyworth life, was transformed in the late 1960s and the 1970s. From 1894 to the end of the Second World War, most Keyworth children started and finished their education at Keyworth Board School. The 1944 Education Act introduced the 11-plus exam by which academic children went to grammar schools and the rest to secondary modern schools. After 1945 grammar school children went to schools in West Bridgford and Nottingham, but secondary modern school children remained at Keyworth School until 1956. In that year Lutterell Secondary Modern School was opened in West Bridgford and Keyworth Board School became a primary school. The rise in population meant that Keyworth School became too small. New primary schools were built — first at Nottingham Road and later at Willow Brook and Crossdale. South Wolds School was opened as a secondary modern school in 1967. When the 11-plus exam was abolished in Nottinghamshire it became a comprehensive school and Keyworth children could, once again, complete their education in the village. The expansion of education in the country as a whole created a need for more teachers and this explains why Mary Ward College came to Keyworth in 1968.

Keyworth Board School

Keyworth Board School was opened in 1874, after bitter opposition from the Anglican Rector of Keyworth. By 1894 much of the hostility had subsided. This was partly due to the conciliatory attitude of the Rev Henry Pratt Ling, who had become Rector of Keyworth in 1878.

The Headmaster in 1894 was Henry D. Neate. He had been appointed in 1890 and was to remain Head until 1921. 'Daddy Neate', as he was known, gave the school stability which contributed to good educational standards. At the turn of the century there were five full time and four pupil teachers. One of the pupil teachers was Miss Deborah Tomlinson, who continued to teach at the school for many years and died as recently as 1982. In 1902 Miss Ethel Davill became a pupil teacher at the school. When she married she became Mrs Ethel Bennett and taught the infants until 1949.

Staff of Keyworth Board School, 1899. Back row: L. Dring, S. B. Price, Mr Folley, D. A. Tomlinson. Front row: Miss Neale, Miss Whalley, Edith Sayers, Miss Bates, Mr H. D. Neate (Headmaster).

Since 1893 the school had provided adult evening classes as well as extra subject classes for the older children. A total of 17 subjects was offered. Tuition was from 7.30 to 9.45 in the evenings. The fee was 2d per week, which was refunded if the pupil was successful in the examination. A government grant was available and the average attendance was 64 persons. 'Daddy Neate' retired in 1921 and continued to play a role in the community. A former pupil, Marjorie Goddard (now Mrs Bradshaw), remembers how he suffered a stroke and was confined to a wheelchair, which was pushed by his wife, and was the subject of a few tricks by his former pupils.

He was succeeded by Mr Kirk, who in turn was succeeded by Mr John Twells, who was Headmaster from 1925 to 1949. Thus two headmasters presided over Keyworth Board School for a total of 55 years. It was during Mr Twells's headship that the school experienced its first major population explosion. At the outset of the Second World War large numbers of evacuees — from Sheffield and later from Great Yarmouth and Nottingham — came to live in Keyworth and the surrounding area. Mrs Gladys Wright was one of the teachers who came with the evacuees from Sheffield to Plumtree School. Full use was made of local halls and meeting places. Stanton Golf Pavilion, the Congregational Lecture Hall and the Methodist Hall were used as addi-

Keyworth School 1950/51
Back row: Maureen Stevenson, Eunice Davinson, Pat Attewell, Marjorie
Snowden, Brenda Richards, Melvis Warr, Shirley Brown.
Middle Row: Stanley Hull, Mr Ridgway (Headmaster), Pat Brumby, Billy Spick,
Brenda Goddard, Terry Swain, Audrey Goddard, John Bingham, Betty Davis,
John Smith.
Front row (standing): Wendy Brumby, June Disney, Eric Elliott, Vivien Disney,
Alec Green, Kathleen Hall, John Marshall, Jean Booth, David Oldham, Rosemary
Mellors, Doris Pownall.
Seated: David Orridge, Derek Redmile, ? Wakerley, Eddie Hart, George Gibson,
John Chappell, John Eggleston.

tional classrooms. The school field was given over to the production of food crops.

The School Log 1 September 1939:
'140 Sheffield children and adults arrived in Keyworth in the afternoon. Received in school and given tea and buns, then billeted in various houses. A scheme sent re: education of children. A welfare committee formed in local First Aid: to be used as clinic'.

School Log 6 October 1939:
'Number on books: Keyworth 199, Sheffield 60, Nottingham 8'.

In 1949 the Headmaster, Mr Twells, and Infant Teacher, Mrs Ethel Bennett, both retired. They were succeeded by Mr Arthur Ridgway and Mrs Gladys

Keyworth County Infants School 1976 (formerly the Board School).

Wright, by which time the teaching staff had decreased to five and the post war population explosion was affecting the very limited school accommodation. In 1952 additional classrooms were being built and the two infant classes with teachers Mrs Annie Mills and Mrs Gladys Wright moved temporarily to the Congregational Lecture Hall.

Both classes were accommodated in two long rows of tables and chairs in the one large room. The outdoor play facilities were almost non-existent and the 'pan lavatories' were approached through the graveyard. It was here that a child narrowly avoided very serious injury when a spike on the entrance gates pierced his neck.

The provision of secondary places at the newly built Lutterell Secondary Modern School in 1956 meant that all children left Keyworth School at the age of eleven and so Keyworth School became Keyworth Primary School. This was to comply with the requirements of the 1944 Education Act. In the same year, a large hall and classroom were built and for the first time large P.E. apparatus was installed.

The continued growth in population in the early 1960s produced a rapid expansion of building in the village. The open fields behind the school which stretched beyond Willow Brook up to Nicker Hill were gradually built upon by George Wimpey and Frank Goulding. Six new classrooms, a dining area and a kitchen completed the school accommodation. However, the school was still overcrowded and between 1964 and 1966 the newly built Nottingham Road School became the temporary Infant School with Gladys Wright as Headmistress and the Selby Lane site became Keyworth Junior School with Mr Ridgway as Headmaster. In 1966 the two schools exchanged sites and, at Selby Lane, Keyworth County Infants School became Nottinghamshire's largest infant school, occupying twelve classrooms.

School life continued apace — a fire in the boiler house, the sudden appearance of a large hole in the playground, thought to be a disused well. A local doctor living opposite the school felt privileged to perform his daily ablutions to the accompaniment of the infants' morning assembly.

In 1974 the Centenary of the School was celebrated by a large exhibition of children's work as well as photographs and memorabilia contributed by local residents, including a pair of handmade boots made by Mr Herbert Mills, who with his son Billy had a cobbler's shop opposite the school on Selby Lane. All pupils and staff were presented with a blue and cream Devonshire ware mug inscribed 'Keyworth Board School 1874–1974'. The following year Mrs Gladys Wright retired and Mrs Sheila Barwick became the last Headteacher of the School.

The entire school buildings and occupants were decked in the national colours of red, white and blue to celebrate the Silver Jubilee of Queen Elizabeth II in 1977. A Silver Jubilee Garden was planted with a silver trowel used by Princess Margaret.

By the early 1980s the rate of new development in Keyworth had decreased, along with the rate of population expansion. The post war 'bulge' had been educated, grown up and in many cases left the village, and the extra school provisions made in the previous decades were now no longer needed. However, the sadness felt when it was announced that the Keyworth Infant School was to close on 17 July 1985 was shared by the whole village community. Despite determined opposition by many individuals, everything in the school from piano to pencil was sorted and colour coded to be either discarded or to be amalgamated with Nottingham Road Junior School, to become Keyworth Primary School. Amid continuing controversy, the school was demolished in December 1986. Mr Horace Murden summed up the feelings of the whole village in his letter to the Nottingham Evening Post on 6 December 1986:

'Sad echo of the Old School Bell'

'With a sadness I saw the demolition start at our Council School on Monday. My first day at the school was on 13 January 1906. I remember watching the mill sails in action some 150 yards away. My thoughts went back to my old classmates. Most of these have now died. How we ran to get into our lines before the school bell stopped ringing. Happy days.

Private Education

A minority of Keyworth parents have preferred a private or denominational education for their children. Most privately educated children have attended day schools in Nottingham or Loughborough or boarding schools in other parts of England. But, for a time, there was a private school in Keyworth.

Selby Lodge School was a small establishment offering education for six to ten pupils whose ages ranged from five to eleven years, with the option of remaining until the age of fourteen. The school was held in a private house at the far right hand side of Selby Lane, still known today as Selby Lodge. The house has since been renovated and many mature trees have been removed from the garden. A former pupil, Mr Peter Coke, remembers a small spinney at the side of the house and a large gorse-covered field at the rear.

The house was occupied by three sisters. Miss Fanny Taylor and Mrs Marks were teachers in the school and the third sister was a Mrs Gertrude Watts. The school was upstairs at the back of the house and all pupils were taught individually in the same classroom. There were no facilities for sport or music, but good manners and politeness were insisted upon. The school fees were 2s 6d per week — payable termly in advance. The school started some time after 1910 and closed in the 1930s.

Primary Schools

The continual influx of young families into Keyworth in the 1960s and 1970s necessitated the building of new schools. Selby Lane School was supplemented, first by Nottingham Road School and later by Willowbrook and Crossdale.

As already noted, Nottingham Road School had an unusual beginning. For two and a half years from 1964 to 1966 it was Keyworth Infants School with Mrs Gladys Wright as its Headmistress. During this time, the second phase of building took place and it was only when Mr Ridgway moved the Junior School from Selby Lane in 1966 that it became Keyworth Junior School.

Mr Ridgway retired in 1969 after 20 years teaching in Keyworth. He was succeeded by Mr John Hartley, who was to remain Head for the next 16 years. His assemblies, often based on his war experiences, are still remembered by past pupils.

During this time the school grew rapidly and at its maximum had just over 550 children on roll. There were sometimes 50 children in a class. The school hall, the staffroom and a room at South Wolds School were used as extra classrooms. At one time 475 children stayed for school dinners and Mrs A. M. Priestley arranged for them to be served in three shifts.

It was a very busy and active school with a dedicated and hardworking staff. The Deputy Heads were Mrs I. M. Thurland followed by Miss G. Catchpole. A great feature of this time was the success of the music and, in particular, the Guitar Band under Mrs Margaret Glaves. They gave many concerts, made two records and broadcast on radio and TV. The choir was also successful and they won their class at the Nottingham Music Festival. The football and netball teams were successful in the Rushcliffe Junior League and two girls reached county standard in basketball. There were clubs for chess, Scottish dancing, gymnastics, table tennis and badminton. Cycling proficiency tests were introduced and all children had swimming lessons at the new Keyworth pool.

In 1985 numbers had fallen both at the Infant and Junior Schools. Mrs Sheila Barwick, Headmistress of Selby Lane Infants School, was given the task of amalgamating the two schools, which became known as Keyworth Primary School. It was a complex operation, carried out efficiently. Mrs Barwick retired in 1988 and was succeeded by the present Headteacher, Mr Paul Aspinall. Rooms which were formerly classrooms have become areas for specialist use. There are now separate areas for TV, music, design and technology, special needs and a thriving toddler group. A parents association known as 'Friends of Keyworth Primary School' was formed six years ago and has organised a wide range of social and fund-raising activities for the school. Outdoor and environmental education are a particular feature of the school today.

Willowbrook School opened on 3 September 1969. It was built as a direct result of the rapid building expansion of Keyworth and immediately relieved the pressure on Keyworth Infants School and Nottingham Road Junior School.

Initially, it provided open plan accommodation for 150 pupils aged five to nine years in five classes. Mr Robert Howarth was the first headmaster, with a teaching staff of five. On the opening day the grounds had yet to be planted with shrubs and bushes, much of the school equipment had not arrived and the drains became blocked. In December 1972 Mr Howarth was succeeded by Mr R. F. W. Robinson. The number on roll was now 291 pupils aged between five and eleven years. During his headship, together with the enthusiasm of the staff and the expertise of Mrs Janet van der Colff in particular, the school's musical tradition was developed, producing musicals such as *Oliver*.

The school has nurtured an enduring interest in animals and nature, begun and continued by Mrs Mabel Brown. In June 1973 a pond was excavated in the animal area and over the years many animals, birds and fish have made their home at Willowbrook. These include guinea fowl, which provided impromptu accompaniment to many concerts, a peacock and peahen purchased in 1977 to commemorate Queen Elizabeth's Silver Jubilee, who were aptly named Philip and Elizabeth, and a pair of golden pheasants called Jim and Doreen after the school caretakers, Mr and Mrs J. Booth.

By the mid 70s the school population had peaked to well over 300. There were ten class teachers with classes being held in the Dining Room, Infant Resource Area and Junior Craft Area. On 1 September 1977 the present Headteacher, Mr Michael Atkinson, succeeded Mr Robinson and in January 1978 Mrs Jillian Elliot became Deputy Headteacher, replacing Mr Griffiths.

Crossdale Drive School 1992. Rushcliffe Borough Council's Award 'Towards a Better Environment'.

The school's established interests in nature and music were furthered under this dual leadership.

In February 1985 the school held a Giant Auction inspired and organised by Mrs Mabel Brown in response to the worldwide aid appeal for the Ethiopian famine victims.

In 1987 the whole school was saddened by the early death of Mrs Jillian Elliot, whose musical and artistic talents were greatly missed. The new Deputy Head was Mr Ian Jenkinson. December 1992 saw the retirement of Mrs Irene Wakeman, school secretary for 23 years. Fortunately, although the use of her typing skills has ceased, that of her musical talents has not and she continues to arrange and accompany for the choir and concerts. In 1994 the number on roll is 242.

Like Willowbrook, Crossdale Drive School was housed in an open plan building. It opened in 1974 with 166 pupils; it grew rapidly to a maximum of 296 in 1979 though, as with other schools in Keyworth, the changing pattern of families and the lessening birthrate have brought a fall in numbers since. Deliveries of equipment were late and on the first day there were no chairs!

For the first ten years the school was under the direction of Miss P. Graham, who established it as an important part of the local educational scene. The children's maroon and grey uniform became familiar to all. Activities involving the children in the life of the locality have always been prominent. By 1976 the school was participating in the Keyworth Schools Arts Festival

35

and a tradition of dramatic productions and musical activities (*Oliver* and *Evacuees* among the most recent) was established. In 1992 the school received an award from Rushcliffe Borough Council for its project 'Towards a Better Environment'.

Miss Graham retired in 1984 and was followed by Mrs J. Osborn. Mrs Osborn left in 1987 for a higher post with Nottinghamshire Education Authority, to be succeeded by the present Headteacher, Mr C. Conway.

Over the years there have been problems — some humorous. There was an unsuccessful attempt to take part of the school field for building. One person tried to claim a right of way across school property, not realising that the footpath had been diverted. The weather has sometimes had its effect — Miss Oxby once took to travel by tractor under snowy conditions.

The atmosphere of the school is that of a family. Three people have worked in the school since its opening — two teachers, Mrs P. Smith and Miss V. Oxby, and the secretary, Mrs J. Stocker. Many more have made enormous contributions to the school and the education of its pupils. The school's roots and memories may not yet be as long as those of older institutions, but at Crossdale Drive one can see a typical part of the recent history of Keyworth since its expansion began — local history in the making.

South Wolds School

South Wolds School began its life as a secondary modern school on 10 January 1967, in response to the urgent need for secondary places in South Nottinghamshire. Mr Colin Cawthorn was appointed Headmaster. The first intake totalled 146. Additional first year pupils from Keyworth Primary and ManversPrimary in Cotgrave entered the school in September 1967. In 1968, the school presented its first dramatic production, a one act play *The Price of Coal*. The title seems ironical in considering recent developments in the mining industry. The following year South Wolds became the venue for the Duke of Edinburgh Award Scheme Presentations.

School Log 27 March 1969
'The Duke of Edinburgh arrived by helicopter at 12.10 p.m., landing on the Hockey Field at the west side of the school. He toured the displays and exhibitions of the award scheme and was entertained to luncheon in the Public Library. He expressed great pleasure in his visit and showed much interest in the school and its future.'

With the abolition of the 11-plus examination, South Wolds became South Wolds Comprehensive School in September 1970. By September 1975 the number on roll had risen to 1149, necessitating extra school accommodation. Sixth Form and Humanities Blocks were begun in 1976, but despite this a second year class was housed in Selby Lane Infant School.

The school's Concert Band under the dual leadership of Mr Chris

South Wolds School 25th anniversary, 10 January 1992. Alan Langton, headteacher, and Colin Cawthorne, former headteacher, cutting the cake.

McDouall and Mr Geoff Bocking became well-known. It played for the local celebrations of Queen Elizabeth's Silver Jubilee and travelled to France for the official Twinning Ceremonies between Keyworth and Feignies. From 1976 it became an established part of the annual Keyworth Schools Music Festival in which South Wolds and its feeder primary schools took part.

1978 saw with sadness the early death of Mrs Linda Thomas, one of the original teaching staff. Her memorial tablet is at the entrance to the school hall. However, as the School Log for 24 June 1978 records, 'her true memorial will rest in the hearts and minds of hundreds of former pupils who have good cause to remember her guidance and kindness in the formative years'

In 1981 Mr Cawthorn was succeeded by Mr Alan Langton as Headmaster, with a staff of 73 and 1277 pupils. As a direct recommendation of the Warnock Report, South Wolds saw the integration of pupils with physical disabilities into mainstream education in 1982. South Wolds admitted three such pupils. Ramps and lifts were installed and a full time care assistant was appointed. Mr Langton commented on the dual success of the initiative: for the physically disabled pupil, 'academic success along with a growth of confidence and independence in the hurly-burly of a mainstream school' and for the whole school, 'a daily awareness of disability, offering a helping hand and witnessing colossal determination and bravery'.

In 1992 the whole school was shocked by the very sudden death of Mr Brent Ashley, who taught History and Economics at South Wolds for thirteen years and contributed so much to the varied life of the school.

37

Mary Ward College 1973. Reproduced with the permission of the Nottingham Evening Post. ©*TBF*

A number of former pupils have also suffered untimely death or injury. In particular Keyworth remembers Colette Aram, who was murdered in 1983. Kevin Woodford was badly wounded when serving with the Royal Marines in the Falklands War in 1982 and was subsequently presented with a car by the people of Keyworth. More recently, Royal Marine Robert Pike was accidentally killed in Norway in 1993.

1994 sees the retirement of Mr Alan Langton. He has played a much appreciated role in the life of Keyworth and established, on the foundations laid by Mr Colin Cawthorn, South Wolds School's reputation for academic success. He is succeeded by Mrs Sheila Roser, who inherits a teaching staff of 62 and 1056 pupils.

Mary Ward College

Mary Ward College was administered by the Sisters of Loreto, who had been founded by Mary Ward — an independent and forward-thinking nun who lived in the seventeenth century. It began its short life in 1967 in a former boys' public school at Beaumont near Windsor, because the new campus at Keyworth was not ready.

The new College Campus resembled a First World War battlefield when it opened in Keyworth in October 1968. At one point the intake reached 540 students but the halls of residence accommodated only 225. The remainder were based in Keyworth and the surrounding locality. Many Keyworth families shared their homes with the students. Nearly half of the students came from Northern Ireland and the contacts between the students and Keyworth people helped to foster understanding between the two communities. Many families still keep in touch with their former guests. The remainder of the students were from a variety of backgrounds. There were some nuns who were acquiring qualifications after teaching for a number of years and there was a growing number of mature students, most of whom were local people.

By 1970, when the college was officially opened by Princess Anne, the college buildings were completed. The Beaumont Assembly Hall was named after the college's early venue. The Chapel had a magnificent stained glass window on the North Wall depicting the Annunciation and the Visitation.

The local community became integrated into the life of the college. Many local people were employed there in administrative and domestic roles. The College Chapel became the Church for the Catholic community in the village and Beaumont Hall was the venue for dramatic productions produced by Mr Donald Holmes and for the Annual College Ball. There was also a playgroup organised by the students.

The planned closure was deeply felt, but, at least, staff were given over two years' notice before the college finally closed in 1977. There is a permanent reminder of the part played by Mary Ward College in the Memorial Gates leading onto the Playing Fields from Nottingham Road. They were donated by the Sisters of Loreto in memory of their time spent in Keyworth.

The Pre-School Child

By the late 1960s the continuing expansion of Keyworth created the necessity for some educational provision for the pre-school child. With the absence of any LEA nursery provision, this saw the emergence of the playgroup movement. This was prior to the existence of the PPA (Pre-school Playgroup Association), each group being privately formed by interested persons and held in public halls or private homes, their aim being to provide safe, meaningful play experience for the pre-school child.

The first group, formed by Mrs Lock at her bungalow on Selby Lane, later moved to larger premises in the newly built Village Hall where the supervisor for many years was Mrs Lee. After almost 30 years, and under a variety of titles and supervisors, the playgroup closed in July 1994.

The second group was founded by teacher Mrs Margaret Harvey and held in a specially constructed nursery classroom for 20 children at the rear of her home in Rose Grove (formerly the telephone exchange). It was called Orchard House Nursery School and the designing and making of creative learning equipment became the inspiration for the formation of the educational toy manufacturers, Orchard Toys. When this occurred the nursery moved to Burnside Hall, Plumtree, under the leadership of Mrs Rita Wain until her sudden death in 1992. The present supervisor is Mrs Susan Karimjee.

The Beaver Playgroup, held at 2 Delville Avenue, emerged in 1967 under the supervision of Mrs A. Moore and Mrs B. Jackson, joined one year later by Mrs M. Allen. After approximately six years Mrs N. Newman became supervisor and, two years later, moved the playgroup to new premises in a neighbouring village.

Mrs Mary Bradshaw converted two semi-detached houses on the Fairway into the one house from which she ran her playgroup.

1969 saw the formation of the South Wolds Playgroup — more popularly known as the Parochial Hall Playgroup — the latter being the venue for the 25 years of its existence. It is a parent run group, the present supervisor being Mrs Angela Forman, with a staff of three helpers.

In February 1971, under the leadership of the Minister, Miss June Davis, the United Reformed Church formed a playgroup held in its newly opened Webster hall, from which the group derived its unofficial title. The first supervisor of this Christ Church (Keyworth) Playgroup was Mrs Lona Green, succeeded by Mrs Margaret Prebble in 1973 and Mrs Daphne Butler in 1975, who with assistant supervisor Mrs Val Eggleston and a group of long serving staff ran the playgroup until July 1994. The Constitution and Management of the playgroup was revised from September 1994 as the Webster Hall Playgroup to continue with Mrs Mel Cottee and Mrs Sally Gregor as joint supervisors.

Keyworth in the 1990s has fewer pre-school children than in the previous two decades, when the PPA provided a much needed community service. There are no longer any playgroups held in private homes and only two groups in public halls in Keyworth. However, September 1995 sees the first LEA provision for the under fives. A 40 place nursery unit will be opening at Keyworth Primary School. It marks the beginning of a new era of education in Keyworth.

Chapter 5

Health and Welfare

One hundred years ago Keyworth was a largely self-contained community. By present-day standards material conditions of life were low but on the whole poverty was not extreme. Some 40 of the village population of 700–800 were listed as property owners in 1895. In the nineteenth century there was a wide range of businesses within the village serving the needs of the community: the range at some time included tailors, dressmakers, and a bonnetmaker as well as the usual shops for food and the craftsmen necessary for rural life — builders, blacksmiths, joiners and others.

Hard work was the order of the day for all, but this and the neighbourliness of a community where everyone knew everyone else, and most were related to each other in some way, meant that those in difficult circumstances were regularly helped by others. Whether Keyworth lost something through the absence of a benevolent lord of the manor or gained by being a community of independent men and women is difficult to say. But the community was held together by self-help and mutual support. In the early twentieth century there was a police presence (the first police house was at 3 Selby Lane) but crime was low. The district was shocked when Elias Torr, of Hickling Pastures, shot and killed his daughter Mary Ann in 1899 and was subsequently executed, but such things were rare to the point of being virtually unheard of. Social activities provided occasional breaks from the daily grind, which was the lot of almost all from starting work at the age of about 13 years until old age.

The health of the community seems to have been generally good. Water came from wells and the village pump and must have been satisfactory. Open drainage in the streets, lack of sewerage facilities and less than hygienic methods of sewage disposal do not seem to have been a great health hazard. Sewage, when not disposed of by householders themselves, was collected once a week by a carrier, who took the full bucket and left an empty one at each house. One resident remembers the odour outside the fish and chip shop when the carrier called there for his lunch!

There seem to have been no epidemics, except for the annual cases of children's ailments. This was in spite of the poor take-up of vaccination against smallpox: folk were very suspicious of this practice. But there seem to have been no cases of smallpox in Keyworth this century. As in other rural areas child mortality was relatively low: those reaching adulthood could have a

'Seeking Relief'

good life expectancy. Clearly this community did not experience the destitution and slum conditions seen in towns.

There did exist a service of support for the poor and needy, although it would be considered inadequate today. This took the form of the Poor Law Unions which had replaced the ancient system whereby parishes were responsible for their own poor. Keyworth fell in the Bingham Union: Union funds, dependent on a poor law rate raised by each parish, provided support for the needy of the area covered by the Union. The poor law rate in Keyworth, calculated on the rateable value of property, was 1½d in the pound in 1895. Each Union supported a workhouse, to provide basic accommodation and board, but these were regarded as a last resort. Each parish had to appoint an overseer of the poor: from 1895 this was a duty of the Parish

Council at its annual meeting. The Union system lasted until 1930, when the Unions were dissolved and their functions taken over by local authorities.

Being dependent on the poor law system, and especially being admitted to the workhouse, was considered a social disgrace, to be hidden from other members of the community if at all possible. Keyworth complained to the Union Governing Board in 1893 that the overseer paid out poor relief in his shop: presumably this was considered too public a place. This led the relieving officer to arrange that the shopkeeper 'would allow the paupers to enter his home by the front door' and would use his private room for paying out relief.

In these circumstances it was natural that many turned to various other schemes for helping each other in times of need, usually involving a high degree of self-help. A benefaction of 1786 provided a small amount of interest which was distributed to poor widows at Whitsuntide annually. More important, the Parish Enclosure Settlement of 1798 set aside a plot of land to be rented as allotments to residents of the parish, the income to be for the benefit of the poor of the parish. These allotments still exist at the corner of Selby Lane and Willow Brook — the only plot of land in the parish apart from churchyards that has not changed ownership or use since 1798. Originally under the jurisdiction of the Overseers and Churchwardens, these allotments were transferred to the Parish Council on its formation in 1894: the council appointed and still appoints a trust of four members to administer them. The proceeds have at various times been used to assist individual residents who are in financial need, to help support the education of village children and, more recently, to give support to village charitable organisations, such as Keyworth Community Concern.

But a century ago it was the friendly societies which were the most extensive form of welfare insurance. Of these the best documented is the Plumtree Sick Club, formed in 1830 and only finally disbanded in 1992. Its members met on the first Monday of each month at the Griffin Inn. It eventually owned six cottages on Nottingham Road, Keyworth and some ground used as allotments. The cottages, now modernised, are still in existence: the allotments have been sold to Rushcliffe Borough Council, who have promoted the building of the small houses suitable for first-time buyers, among others, which now form Barnett Close. (This name commemorates a Mr Joseph Barnett, who was allotted this land under the settlement of 1798.) The Sick Club had strict rules:

Rule 2   If any member shall enter the room the worse for liquor, swear, take the name of God in vain, promote gaming, lay wagers, or say anything respecting any Member of his family, which have a tendency to cause disputes, he shall forfeit 5s 0d for the first offence, 10s 0d for the second, and shall be excluded for the third, if within a year of each other.

Rule 11   No person shall be admitted a Member of this Society who is above 40, or under 15 years of age, unless he be an official.

Rule 28   If any Member shall lead such a dissipated course of life as, in the opinion of the Committee, will be likely to impair his health, and render him a burden to the Society, he shall be fined ten shillings, and if he still persists in such a course, or refuses to pay the forfeit, he shall be excluded.

But if members were disabled by illness or accident they could receive £1 per week for three months and 10s 0d per week thereafter indefinitely, as long as they could not work. These allowances were not ungenerous at the time. Subscriptions to the club obviously increased as time went on — 1s 6d per month in 1926 and 3s 0d per month in 1971.

The Oddfellows, associated with a country-wide fellowship, the Independent Order of Rechabites (a temperance organisation), formed a similar society in the village. This club flourished for a time, but eventually it collapsed, apparently owing to a shortage of funds resulting from too heavy and frequent demands from members. This club too owned six houses at one time. In 1905 there were also mentioned in the valuation lists for the parish a Keyworth Club, owning six houses and one shop, and a Bunny Club, owning six houses. In 1914 there is a record stating that Flawforth Lodge Friendly Society owned six brick and slate cottages, with two bedrooms each, in Keyworth: one was in Commercial Road. The cottages of all these were let at reasonable rents, presumably to club members in need of housing. To what extent all these clubs existed at the same time, or overlapped with each other or covered residents of other parishes, needs further research, but it is clear that life was considerably eased for those in need by such associations.

The overwhelming majority of claims on these clubs, if not the total number, came from people unable to carry on their work because of medical conditions due to illness or accident. This encourages enquiry as to how those needs were met in medical terms. In the absence of a comprehensive health service, 'free at the point of access' (although Lloyd George's National Insurance Act of 1911 leading to the panel system made a beginning in that direction), medical treatment was available only for payment. It is true, however, that doctors often omitted to charge patients whom they knew to be in straitened financial circumstances. Keyworth had a resident doctor — Arthur William Hare — until 1902, when Dr A. L. Rhind, from Ireland, arrived; he was to stay for 46 years, becoming a much loved and respected member of the village community. Mr Henry Lacey met him with his horse cab at Plumtree Station and the whole village turned out to greet him at his temporary accommodation. He moved first to Wysall Lane and later to the house between the Methodist Church and the Plough Inn, on Selby Lane, which became known as the Doctor's House. He shared some duties with Dr Hunter, of Ruddington, and for some years lived at Ruddington, though

Plumtree Sick Club Cottages, Nottingham Road.

travelling to Keyworth every day to visit patients. Eventually, in 1938, he moved to a newly built house and surgery (now the optician's premises) in Bunny Lane.

To begin with, most of his patients who were unable to go to the surgery could be visited on foot: more distant ones were reached by horse. Soon Dr Rhind had a bicycle and a pony and trap, then a motor cycle, later an Austin 7 car. Surgery was held daily at 12 noon. After this Dr Rhind would collect messages from the Richmonds at Plumtree Post Office. He kept accounts in a day book and sent out bills quarterly, with generosity shown, it is said, to those who could not afford to pay. The charge was 1s 0d for a visit to the surgery and 2s 6d for a home visit. As was the custom of general practitioners at the time, he dispensed his own medicines, which he always wrapped in white paper and sealed with wax.

Many folk still remember Dr Rhind. Some saw him as very quiet and polite: others remember him as stern and tall, very autocratic and very strict. One resident says 'all I can remember is waiting in the surgery and the silence except for the gas fire': another tells that on going to work one morning he fell and broke his leg. Dr Rhind came to him in his pyjamas.

In May 1918 a meeting took place at Normanton House to launch the Plumtree and District Nursing Association. For an annual subscription of 4s 0d and an additional fee of 15s 6d for midwifery, the employment of a professional nurse for the area was ensured. Treatment was to be free for old-age pensioners. This was the only such provision until the coming of the NHS. It proved a very valuable service. In 1926 Nurse Turner made 2,490 visits and attended 14 deliveries. She was awarded an extra £10 salary because of her kindly personal interest. In 1937 the nurse had a telephone installed, to supplement the notice board outside her lodgings. The service was supported by money-raising efforts — jumble sales, church collections and concerts. Once Keyworth Male Voice Choir was asked to perform on a Sunday, but to limit their repertoire to suitable sacred music!

The biggest change came in 1948. Not only did Dr Rhind retire, to be replaced by Dr Manson Russell, but on 5 July of that year the NHS was established. Dr Russell writes:

'The medical team for the first four years consisted of one nurse–midwife and myself. This was for a population of 2,500 based on Keyworth and district. Some patients lived as far away as Nether Broughton and East Leake.

'The surgery was based on my house on Bunny Lane. Surgeries were held morning and evening each day, including Saturdays. Wednesday was normally a half day, but cover had to be given for emergencies.

'The NHS, with its free treatment and, at that time, free medicine was revolutionary in its effects. Also, with more money, the medical advances of the last 45 years have been enormous.

'The ears of children afford one spectacular example. In 1948, and for centuries before, children had commonly suffered from chronic discharging ears. The advent of the NHS meant that no longer did we hear people say "we didn't go to the doctor — we couldn't afford to", and useless patent medicines were less often used. With good medical attention and, co-incidentally, the huge impact of the coming of penicillin and other antibiotics, children's ear infections and mastoiditis became easily treatable conditions and mastoid operations very rare.

'There have been big advances in maternity services. In 1948 many babies were born at home. Our nurse–midwife was well trained and very competent. When troubles arose, together in the homes we undertook forceps deliveries under anaesthesia and dealt with other hair-raising emergencies which would, rightly, be dealt with in hospital today. One might call this age one of "heroic midwifery". But with mainly hospital admissions now something has been lost, because when home deliveries went smoothly — the majority — it was much happier for the new mother to be at home with her husband and family in familiar surroundings.

'In the Keyworth practice one doctor became two in 1952 — Dr Stevenson came — and three in 1962 — with Dr Annesley. The surgery moved to Dr Annesley's new home on Selby Lane. Back-up staff increased and the new Health Centre opened in 1970. Clinics operating in village halls moved there and a new concept of Family Practice, now called Primary Care, had begun.'

The new centre of which Dr Russell writes had a wing for baby clinics and for such services as vaccinations, in which another new arrival, Dr

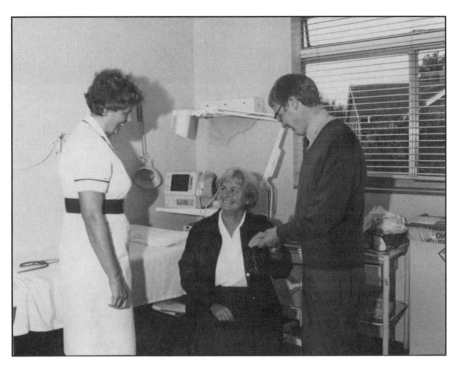

Keyworth Health Centre 1994.

Jenkinson, took a great interest. Emphasis on the prevention of infectious diseases by programmes of immunisation has continued since the Second World War and the coming of the NHS. In addition to immunisations already standard, those against mumps, measles and rubella were added in 1988, and against the Hib organism, which causes a form of meningitis, in 1992. By 1994 99% of the children in Keyworth were covered against all these illnesses. The treatment of asthma has been revolutionised by the advent of inhaled steroids and better education for sufferers. Special asthma, diabetes and 'well person' clinics have been set up to encourage a healthy life style. All these are run by the practice nurses, who have taken on an ever increasing role in the community health care.

Fundholding started in April 1992 and the Keyworth practice was one of the first wave in the country to take up the scheme: indeed Dr Annesley and Dr Andrew Wood, who joined the practice in 1983, took part in a documentary and discussion programme on the subject for the BBC's *Panorama*.

Help and self-help for the sick and needy have never been the only charitable activities in Keyworth. The churches, for example, have always contributed to their own missionary and social work nationwide and overseas: between the wars the British Legion, which cares for victims of the two World Wars and, more recently, of all wars in which British citizens are involved, founded a flourishing branch in the village. The influx of population in the 1960s and 1970s meant that all sorts of sports and special interest societies sprang up. Some of these exist solely for the raising of funds for charitable purposes, such as Cancer Research, the Royal National Lifeboat Institution: others often organise fund-raising events in addition to their programme for club members. Village-wide collections for the Salvation Army, Christian Aid, Oxfam and similar international charities are now annual events.

Within the village the WRVS has been active. It organised for some time the 'Meals on Wheels' service, which has now been taken over by the County Council. There is also a 'Books on Wheels' service still run by the WRVS: these two services, together with the system of home helps, act to some extent as a means of contact with the elderly and housebound.

There also seemed to be a need for a social club for older residents of the village. The Darby and Joan Club was started in 1958: its aim was to provide friendship, chat, games, music (in those days there were people who could play the piano) and tea and home-made cakes. Later outings were included. Two-car families were very rare then, so that any who could help, members of the club or not, were roped in to provide transport when necessary. This club still flourishes and is now called the 'Over Sixties Club'.

In 1974, at the time of the three-day week and the power cuts, the Parish Council inaugurated the Keyworth and District Community Concern Committee, initially to monitor cases of hardship among the housebound: it has now became a permanent feature of village life. It was responsible for founding the Tuesday Club for the elderly disabled, which meets weekly and provides a social outlet for some who have difficulty in leaving their homes. It is also responsible for the Community Bus, which is available for hire for various groups, as well as providing a service to transport the elderly or disabled to the shops or to different functions. Recently a Citizen's Advice Centre has been established. The advent of the Rotary Club and the Inner Wheel has also strengthened charitable work in the village.

By contrast with a century ago, Keyworth is a generally prosperous community, and there is little deprivation apparent. The atmosphere is more suburban than rural, with the result that a higher standard of social service provided by the authorities rather than by neighbours is expected. Horizons have broadened: families are scattered in different parts of the country; travel to the towns, to other parts of the country and abroad is now commonplace. But there may be some changes on the debit side. The problems of urban society, especially where crime is concerned, have not left Keyworth unscathed.

For many years the lot of the Keyworth policeman had been a happy one. He was not very well paid but he was respected. He wore a serge tunic with black buttons and serge trousers. He had a best tunic with an elaborate row of silver buttons and a lamp. The uniform with its high-necked tight collar was suitable in winter but very uncomfortable in summer. The two big events for the village bobby were the Keyworth Show and the Armistice Day parade. He dealt with domestic disputes and petty crime: he investigated burglaries and checked the farmers' stock registers. This somewhat nostalgic picture is no more. There is no longer an official police house: it has been replaced by a police point. The policeman is more often to be seen in a car, though there has been a trend recently towards doing the beat on foot. Though Keyworth has fewer problems of crime than inner cities, there have been ram raids on shops and robberies from a bank and a Building Society. Anxieties have been felt in the community concerning the general increase in crime and anti-social behaviour: car crime and petty vandalism have been particular problems. This has resulted in the formation of Neighbourhood Watch schemes which now cover a large part of the area. These are fully backed by the four police officers who between them cover Keyworth and surrounding districts. In spite of any debit side, Keyworth is still very fortunate in its strong sense of neighbourliness and the community spirit shown by the large number of sporting, charitable, special interest and other social groups which flourish in the village.

Chapter 6

Sport

The growth of the village in the early 1960s introduced new organised sports to the local community such as bowls, tennis and table tennis. Cricket and football had dominated the sporting scene for many years previously.

Cricket

A cricket club has existed in Keyworth for over 120 years. Cricket was originally played on the Rectory Field until the 1870s, when it was played on a field on Bunny Lane immediately behind the present Davills' (Greenhays) Farm. The move to Bunny Lane is explained in an article which appeared in the *Countryside Magazine* in 1957. The author was J. Hallam, who was born in Keyworth in 1866. Commenting on the struggle that followed the passing of the School Board Act in 1870 he wrote, 'This brought about another change in the life of the village. The Rector (Rev Potter), being so incensed at the defeat, placed a ban on all Free Churchmen entering the Rectory Field where the village cricket matches were played and this led to another club being started with a ground on Bunny Lane'.

An early agreement between William Davill and Keyworth Cricket Club, dated 4 May 1885, showed the rental to be five pounds per annum. It was signed by John Tyler, Joseph Tomlinson, Harry Pike, Thomas Disney and Sam Price. A photograph of the village cricketers in that same year included five Pikes, three Simpsons and two Tomlinsons plus J. Armstrong, J. Tyler and M. Wright. Access to the cricket field was via the farmyard on the village side of the farmhouse, which was built in the 1890s.

Keyworth became one of the best village teams in the county after their move to Bunny Lane. Many of the players achieved fame beyond the village border and it is said that the village turned out no fewer than forty professionals, coaches and so on. Several played cricket for Nottinghamshire, namely Thomas, Walter and William Attewell, Arthur Pike, Thomas Simpson and Matthew William Wright. John Bickley (b.1819), a native of Keyworth, had earlier played for the county and England in the late 1840s and early 1850s.

William 'Dick' Attewell (b. 18 December 1861) is the most famous of all Keyworth cricketers. Perhaps the first indication of his future potential came at the age of twelve when he obtained a hat trick for Keyworth School v

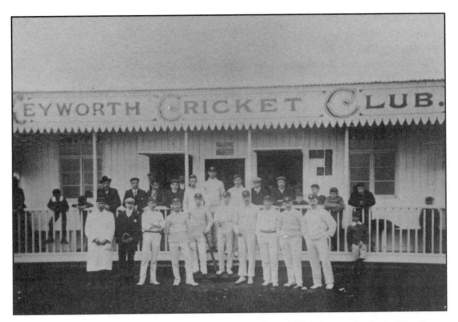

Keyworth Cricket Club, Bunny Lane Ground c.1908. Players included in the photograph are 'Jack' Armstrong (top centre) with Edgar Pike to his right, Jack Attewell (front, second from right) and Henry Hebb (far right)

Plumtree School! It is said that he was quickly re-christened 'Dick' because the Nottinghamshire team had its full complement of 'Williams'. He dominated the Nottinghamshire bowling attack for a longer period of time than any other bowler in the long history of the club, taking 100 wickets in a season on five occasions and 1308 wickets in all, from 1881 to 1900, at an average of 15.51. He also scored 5781 runs for the county at an average of 15.09. He played for England in ten Test Matches, touring Australia on three occasions, and was also on the staff at Lords from 1881 to 1903 playing 53 first class matches for the MCC.

He was born on Old Lane (Elm Avenue), the son of Samuel and Deborah (née Disney), and later married Fanny Hornbuckle living on Main Street. He was a butcher by trade and died in Long Eaton in 1927 on the eve of his 66th birthday.

William Davill died in 1920 and his son Ernest 'Dar' Davill took over the farm. In 1921 the club was fielding two teams in the South Notts League but after the league got into financial difficulties in the early 1920s they resorted to playing friendly matches and by 1928 they also fielded a Thursday XI.

During this period Harry Henson (b.1915) who, like many of hisgeneration, played both cricket and football for the village, lived on Blind Lane (Commercial Road). His mother used to prepare the cricket teas and he recalls having to carry buckets of water from the Stockwell Pump in The

51

Square to the Bunny Lane ground on his bike. The water was boiled on a primus stove in the pavilion. Ernest Davill's daughter Gwen recalls the players helping themselves to apples, much to her mother's disgust, as they made their way through the farmyard to play or practise cricket. Card schools also used to take place in their hovel, a brick cow shelter used for milking.

The problem of repairs required to the wires protecting the cricket square from cattle was frequently raised at the Annual General Meetings of the club (which were usually held in either the Lecture Hall, National School, Rectory, Council School or Legion House prior to the Second World War). In the 1930s they started to look for a new ground. At the AGM in February 1939 it was finally reported that 'The Bunny Lane Ground was in such a condition that it was unfit for play during season 1939'. As a result Mr W. Gunn and Mr H. Tomlinson then left the meeting to interview Mr Ted Eggleston, the then tenant of the Rectory Field, with a view to renting a portion of the field. This was agreed, with the consent of the Rev Brooker, at a yearly rental of £10, subject to certain conditions which included access only by the Selby Lane entrance. An area of 50 square yards was to be fenced off and Mr H. Hebb loaned a horse for the heavy roller to be brought up from the Bunny Lane Ground on Saturday 25 February 1939, followed by Mr B. Lambert and Rev A. B. Brooker promising to bring the mowing machines on the following Saturday. The pavilion, however, was eventually sold to Mrs E. Davill for £6 in early 1940 and was moved to the farmyard where it remains to this day as one of the farm buildings. The club continued to play on the Rectory Field in 1940, changing in the Legion House in The Square for a donation of fifteen shillings, but at the following year's AGM it was decided to disband the club for the duration of the War with £66, the proceeds from two Gymkhanas organised jointly by the Cricket and Football Clubs with a view to providing a Sports Ground for the village, lying in a bank account.

After the War it was agreed for the Cricket and Football Clubs to use the Rectory Field jointly at a rental of £24 per annum and for the grazing rights to be sub-let to Mr L. 'Tommy' Hebb at £12 per annum.

At the AGM in February 1947 it was decided to use the small room in the National School for changing (a charge of 2s 6d was made) and the Welfare Secretary was instructed to apply for a form from the Food Office, Bingham, to obtain certain necessary rationed goods for providing refreshments for home matches. (This was subsequently refused!)

A temporary wicket on the football pitch was used until a new wicket, 30 yards square, was ready for the 1948 season. The club has continued to play on this field, using the same playing area, to this present day. In February 1948 Messrs W. Gunn, A. J. Tomlinson and H. G. Gray represented the club at the first meeting of the Keyworth Playing Fields Association and in the following year the first pavilion was bought and erected at a cost of £150. This money was initially borrowed from the Parish Council's Playing Field Fund and repaid by holding joint social events with the Football Club.

In 1953 the club represented by Tom Hinchcliffe, Charlie Underwood, Brian Ford, Harry Henson, Ron Armstrong and Alec Bennett won the Lenton

Keyworth Cricket Club First XI, 1992
Back row: Kevin Hitchcock, Robert Baker, Richard Drury, Geoff Baker, David Hillbourne, Stuart Meek.
Front row: John Childs, Tony Newby, Tim Hepburn (Capt.), John Dring, Alex Ball.

United 'Six a Side Cup' played on the Gregory Sports Ground, Lenton, in the presence of a large following of villagers. They continued to play friendly matches until 1956 whenthey fielded two teams in the Notts Amateur League. In that same year a second pavilion was purchased and this was used for changing rooms with the original pavilion being used for teas. Membership of the Notts Amateur League continued until the mid 1960s when they reverted to playing friendly matches again.

In 1973 they became founder members of the South Notts Village League, becoming champions in 1976 and runners up in 1984. They won the Eddie Marshall Knock Out Cup in 1979. In 1980 they also joined the Evening League winning that Knock Out Cup in 1993 when they defeated Plumtree.

In 1981 a new pavilion was built to replace the two older buildings and is shared with the Table Tennis Club.

For season 1994 the club ran three teams. The First XI were champions of Division 1 of the Youngers Village League and are promoted to the Premier Division. The Second XI have been relegated to Division 3. The Evening XI were champions of Division 2 of the Nottingham Evening League and gained promotion to Division 1.

Disney XI, 1910. Back row: Walter, Harry, Ezra, Percy, Arthur. Front row: 'Yankee', Harry, Fred, Arnold, Claude, Alf, Oswald.

Football

The village no doubt had a football club well over 100 years ago but the first evidence of its participation in League Football was in 1905 when 'Keyworth' joined the Notts Alliance League. The other teams in that League in the 1905–06 season were Sneinton, Notts Olympic, Basford United, Daybrook, Nottingham St Andrews, Netherfield Rangers, Burton Joyce, Boots Athletic, Lawrence Athletic, Radcliffe on Trent and Notts Commercial. Keyworth played in the Notts Alliance until 1912 when they were relegated, their fate being decided through having six points deducted (reason not known)! Their highest position during this period was fourth in 1906–07. In those days, up to 1912, the home side was allowed to choose the referee!

The late Horace Murden (1902–1992) was a lifelong Keyworth resident, cricketer, footballer and familiar figure in his tweed hat riding his bike or recounting his vivid memories of Keyworth's past. He recalled teams such as Sneinton, Arnold St Mary's and Netherfield Rangers arriving in the village (on horse-drawn carts) to play football. He said the 'football field' was Holmes Chapel Field, the site of the present Nottingham Road Primary School, the field gate being where the Webster Hall entrance now is. On this ground on Boxing Day 1910 an 'All Disney XI' beat the 'Rest of Keyworth' 3–1.

Horace also remembered football being played opposite the Health Centre on Bunny Lane and on Smiths Meadow, Wysall Lane before 1920. The field on Bunny Lane between the cottages and Davills' Farm was also used for the annual 'Disney fixture'.

In the early 1920s and up to the Second World War the 'football field' was on Selby Lane next to the Charity Allotments and opposite Selby Lodge. In the 1920s Keyworth played in the Nottingham Spartan League, winning the First Division Knock Out Cup in 1925–26 and the Second Division Cup in 1929–30. They used the old Plough Inn for changing rooms, although many of the home team turned out ready changed.

H. G. (Peter) Gray, who was 'Hon. Auditor' for the cricket and football clubs for many years, lived in Willow Brook from 1923 and first played football in 1936. In the late 1920s and early 1930s he remembers 30 to 40 villagers turning up to play a friendly, game after work almost every evening of the week, and being allowed to stand behind the goal in order to retrieve the ball from the allotments. A 'sentry box' was situated just inside the gate on Selby Lane where, in the early 1930s, Arthur Marshall or Ralph Bolton would collect the 3d admission. (Peter used to creep through the hedge in the corner nearest Willow Brook until caught by Beacher Pike!) Harry Henson, who first played football in 1930 and was made an honorary life member of the club in 1967, recalls that, in his early days, those not selected for the team used to play friendly matches in Bob Smith's field opposite Wembley Lodge Farm, Wysall Lane and also on Platt Lane on the same side as the present field but on the other side of the railway.

Immediately before and after the War the club was known as 'Normanton and Keyworth FC', becoming 'Keyworth United' in 1947. After the war it moved to the Rectory Field, sharing the ground with the cricket club and using the British Legion for changing rooms before the erection of the first pavilion in 1949. Keyworth played in the Nottingham Realm League (later Nottingham and District) from the late 1930s to 1950.

The period from 1946 to 1951 was the most successful in the club's history. They won the Realm League Championship in 1948, 1949 and 1950, the Notts Junior Cup in 1948 and the League Knock Out Cup in 1949 before a crowd of 1700 at Meadow Lane on Easter Saturday evening. To illustrate their support in those days, on the following Easter Monday 350 saw them play at Gotham and 300 watched the Reserves play at home to Bunny United.

Season 1950–51 saw them transfer to the Nottingham Spartan League again and under the captaincy of Charlie 'Chuck' Underwood they won the League Championship, Knock Out Cup and the Notts Intermediate Cup. In their 30 league matches they averaged almost six goals per game and scored many more in their cup matches, including 18 in an Intermediate Cup tie against Welbeck Colliery. Jimmy Badder and Carl Husk were prolific goal scorers in that era. An article in the *Football Post* described Keyworth as 'one of the best, if not the best, amateur sides in Nottinghamshire'.

Wrights' buses and/or taxis were used to transport players and supporters to the away fixtures of both the football and cricket teams during this period. This arrangement with Wrights worked very well except for one

Keyworth United Football Club 1950/51.
Back row: Harry Henson, Les Fletcher, Fred Easteal, Jack Foster, John Reeve, Fred
Swanborough, Jack Longworth.
Middle Row: George Finnegan, Jack Kershaw, Jack Petchell, Doug Hardy, Percy
Murden, Mal Astbury, Peter Witcomb.
Front row: Ron Armstrong, Dennis Foster, Carl Husk, Stan Brain, Charlie
Underwood, Jimmy Badder, Jimmy Longworth, Mort Rodgers, Jack Sandy.
Seated at front: Alan Daykin, Robert Woodford (mascot), Billy Longworth.

Second XI cricket match at Parliament Street Methodists in August 1947,
when only five Keyworth players arrived at the ground — through a misun-
derstanding with Mrs Wright and the Secretary the car arranged to take
some of the players did not arrive and these players turned up on the Selby
Lane Ground where Mr L. Bloor, the acting First XI captain, had to utilise
their services owing to several First XI members being absent!

About 1953 the football club's first Youth Team was formed. They first
played on the field where Nottingham Road Primary School is situated and
later on Selby Lane in the field behind Wrights' Garage and the old Doctors'
Surgery. The British Legion was used for changing.

In the autumn of 1955 two large trees, a lime and a horse chestnut, were
felled to make way for the present Juniors' pitch on the Rectory Field. These
trees were situated on the Nottingham Road side well inside the cricket field
of play. The horse chestnut together with a similar tree which still stands

Notts Alliance Champions, 1984/5
Back row: Arthur Oldham (Manager), Alan Collier, Tony Kidd, David Buxton,
Sammy Chapman, Robert Clegg, Dave Collison, Peter Boot.
Front row: Bobby Oldham, Gary Wade, Fred Brown, Dennis Jackson (Capt.),
Robert Marchbank, Dean Parr, Stuart Meek.

near the Selby Lane entrance provided 'conkers' for the school children.

Keyworth United First XI again won the Spartan League Championship in 1974 before transferring to the Notts Alliance, after a 63 year absence, in 1975. They immediately won promotion from Division 2, and again in 1978 when they gained promotion from Division 1 to the Premier Division, also winning the Notts Intermediate Cup for the second time. The Rectory Field was considered unfit for the standard of football in the Premier Division of the Notts Alliance with the result that they moved to their present ground on Platt Lane in October 1978.

Between 1979 and 1989, under the management of Arthur Oldham, Keyworth were Premier League Champions in 1985, after being runners up the previous season, reached four semi-finals of the Notts Senior Cup and played in the FA Vase in 1985–86 and 1986–87.

Many Keyworth born footballers have been on the books of either Nottingham Forest or Notts County over the years. Those who played for the first teams were:

Nottingham Forest: Herbert 'Harry' Pike 1887–91 (11 appearances), Horace Pike 1886–96 (183–52 goals), Arthur Pike 1887–90 (3), John 'Jack' Armstrong 1905–22 (461–10).

Notts County: Thomas Simpson 1902 (7), James Woolley 1912 (3), Alfred Widdowson 1919–28 (141), Robert Woodford 1962 (3), Brian Stubbs 1969–80 (487–21).

Jack Armstrong and Brian Stubbs deserve special mention for their services to their clubs. Jack, who was born on Old Lane in 1884, played both football and cricket for Keyworth. His regular position for Forest was half-back and he was club captain for his final three seasons. His appearance record for Forest was not to be broken until almost 30 years later by Jack Burkitt. He continued to live in Keyworth until shortly before his death in 1963.

Brian Stubbs was born on Park Avenue in 1950. He also played football and cricket for village teams before joining Notts County via Loughborough United and was their captain for two seasons in the mid 1970s. He was a rugged central defender; County gained promotion from the Fourth to the Second Division during his time with the club and only Albert Iremonger and David Needham have made more club appearances than Brian, who still lives in Keyworth.

In season 1994–95 Keyworth United are running three senior teams (First XI Notts Alliance Division 1, Reserves and 'A' XIs in the Nottingham and District Spartan League Premier and First Division) and seven junior teams (under 17s — Notts Youth League and under 14s, 13s, 12s, 11s and 9s in the Young Elizabethan League).

Bowls

Keyworth Bowls Club was formed in 1964 and owes its origin to twelve local enthusiasts who saw the possibility of forming a club when land, including the present site, was earmarked for recreational development.

These twelve were George and Myra Barker, Tom Cross, Frank and Clara Eggleston, Bert Hill, Arthur Kennewell, Joseph Merrick, Ron Schofield, Bella Sharpe and Matt and Nancy Wright.

The first public meeting was held in the Lecture Hall, Nottingham Road, on 24 June 1964, followed by subsequent meetings at members' houses. The 'green' was laid and turfed later that same year and enclosed by 680 privet roots, later to be replaced by the present beech hedging (fetched from Wisbech by Tom Cross) in November 1966.

Club rules were first produced in November 1965 and the 'green' was first used on 7 May 1966. By October of that year there were 32 members.

With the help of other local clubs in the village and a donation from the Keyworth Playing Fields Association, a pavilion was erected at a cost of £1395 and officially opened by the President, Arthur Ford, on 25 April 1968. By 1970 membership had risen to 109, reflecting the local popularity of bowls.

In August 1989 the club held its jubilee celebrations and at the close of the 1993 season a brick extension, to the front of the building, was constructed by club members.

The club enters teams in local leagues and also arranges friendly games

A scene from 1967. In the foreground from the left are: Arthur Kennewell, Jack Reeve, John Reeve, Bob Ramsay, Cyril Marchbank and Wilfred Leech.

and internal competitions. The membership in 1994 was 150 with a waiting list — the highest membership in the country for a club with a single green.

Table Tennis

One day in August 1964, at the local cricket club, three players, Alan Foreman, Trevor Hughes and Des Quigley had the idea of forming a Table Tennis Club, but finding suitable premises proved difficult. However the Parish Church Hall (National School) was made available on a Tuesday evening and 20 people attended an opening night on 29 September ,1964. A committee was formed, a team entered in the Nottingham Institute League and the Keyworth Table Tennis Club was born. After finishing next to bottom in their first season they ran from strength to strength. The following year they ran three teams and five the year after.

The club used the Church Hall for two evenings a week after the first season, one team using the Civil Service Club on Wilford Lane, West Bridgford in 1966–67. From 1967 to 1981 they used the Bowls Pavilion, the building which they had helped to fund. In 1981 the new Table Tennis/Cricket Club pavilion was built on the Playing Fields with money raised by the Keyworth Playing Fields Association. This present pavilion is the envy of many clubs in Nottinghamshire as two matches can be played simultaneously.

In season 1993–94 eleven teams from the club were playing in the Nottingham and District League.

Tennis

Keyworth and District Tennis Club was formed at a public meeting held on 25 January 1965, under the auspices of the Keyworth Playing Field Association using two of the existing four courts that had been opened two years earlier. Club members built their own timber club house shortly afterwards.

In 1974 the present clubhouse was erected and membership grew to as many as 300 over the following years, with around twelve teams of all levels competing in both winter and summer leagues against teams throughout Nottinghamshire. The club has always provided top class coaching, mainly for Junior and Intermediates, using three qualified coaches who are all club members.

Over the years four players — Ruth Hutton, Wendy Footitt, Peter Godber and Clive Parsons — have represented Nottinghamshire at senior county level. In 1994 the club was using four courts and had approximately 160 members.

It is interesting to note that on the original plans for 'Keyworth Recreation Ground' (1948) the possible site for two tennis courts was shown as being on the southern end of the present Village Hall Car Park.

Rugby

Keyworth Rugby Club emerged from a meeting in the Village Hall in February 1976 and made its winning debut against Lowdham Grange in the September. Such was the interest that a second team was formed by the November.

For the 1977 season a home ground was found, Wheatcroft Park, on Bunny Lane using South Wolds School for changing rooms and the Tennis Club for after match refreshment. Most of the club players in those early years were local, many from South Wolds School, but as the club became better known it attracted star names from outside the village, including two county players and an England trialist.

By 1982 the club was looking for a new ground and, thanks to a generous grant from the Sports Council, it was able to purchase the former cricket ground and pavilion at Widmerpool which has been its home to this present day.

Even before the move the club was running four teams. Their most successful season was in 1985–86 when they won the Nottinghamshire Shield.

In 1993 the club realised that it had to develop its own talent and began junior rugby coaching (South Wolds School stopped playing rugby in the early 1980s) and for the 1994–95 season it is fielding five teams including a Junior Fifteen.

Chapter 7

Farming: a changing but continuing occupation

A pproaching Keyworth from Wysall, descending from the escarpment and rounding the bends before reaching Wembley Farm, the eye scans a scene largely unchanged for 200 years.

This landscape, on the south of the village, was created when the ancient three field system with its strips, now fossilised in the corrugations we can see elsewhere in the parish, was destroyed for ever by the enclosure act of 1798. The land was partitioned, enclosed by hedges and the fields so formed were allocated to those whose holdings had previously been dispersed throughout the parish. The pattern of the hedgerows which defined and divided properties is discernible still. It has largely determined the ownership or occupation history during the period of change under consideration here, providing a tangible link with the past. However the relative stability of the pattern conceals a process of change which, over the past 100 years, divides into two parts, before and after the Second World War.

During the years up to and including the 1930s, a period of agricultural depression, the cultivated area of the parish declined and the percentage of arable within this total was halved. This was reversed during the war, since when the area of arable land has continued to increase so that by 1984 there were more ploughed acres than in 1894. Comparisons with conditions subsequent to 1984 are made difficult by the changes in the parish boundary made in that year.

Similar patterns of decline followed by growth are to be seen in the figures for livestock. In the early 1940s there was only a quarter the number of sheep there were in 1894, but by 1984 there were three times as many. For the number of cattle, including cows in milk, there has been less fluctuation. Nevertheless, in 1984 there were twice as many as in 1894. These patterns reflect a response to a combination of economic and political circumstances, though some changes had technological or methodological causes. The disappearance of the horse as an agricultural necessity and its replacement by the tractor is an obvious example. At the beginning of the century nearly 60 horses were solely employed in agricultural tasks; by 1954 this number had dropped to 11. However, throughout this period, the number of horses per 1000 acres was 10-15% above the county average.

An even more dramatic change to the farmyard scene has been the virtual disappearance of the hen. At one time there were over 4000 on Keyworth's

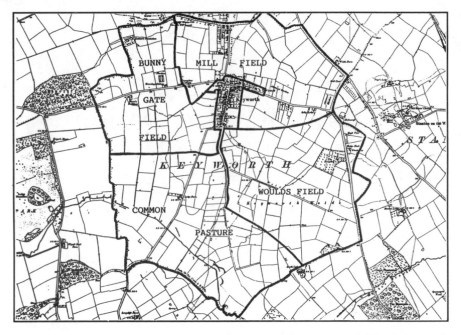

Figure 3: The approximate boundaries of the pre-inclosure open fields of Keyworth Parish. (After Liegh White, 1982 and Notts Archives DD RC 14/15.)

farms, in 1984 only 30, a consequence of the growth elsewhere of 'factory farming'.

In spite of the increased area devoted to crops, Keyworth remained, at least up to 1984, predominantly concerned with livestock farming. Thus its farms supported twice as many dairy cows per 1000 acres as those of the county as a whole. In respect of sheep the difference has been even more dramatic. In 1913 the county average was 394 sheep per 1000 acres, a number which fell to 191 in 1984; the figures for Keyworth were 195 and 951 respectively. As for the number of people engaged in agriculture, this fell from the 50 or more at the turn of the century to under 30 in 1984. Whatever effect this decline had on the economy of the parish, it was completely swamped by the growth of Keyworth in the 1960s. (See chapter 12.)

A trend common to the rest of the country has been the decline in the number of farms in the parish. Thus, in 1894, 35 farms cultivated 1300 acres; in 1984 this acreage was divided between only eleven. At the same time the size of holdings increased: in 1914 of the 34 farms only two were over 100 acres but 70 years later there were six.

Four surveys made during this century supplement these raw statistics. One, carried out just prior to the First World War, was not concerned with agriculture but with raising taxes. This, known as Lloyd George's Domes-

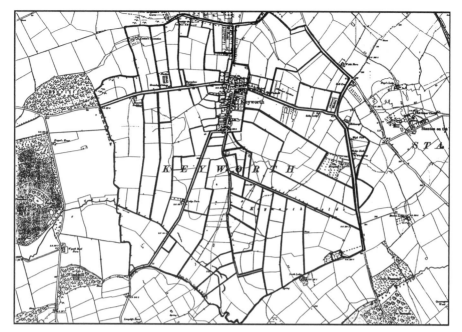

Figure 4: The major property boundaries created under the Enclosure Act, 1798, superimposed on the 20th century OS 6" map reduced to approximately 2½ inches to the mile.

day, provides a comprehensive view of land and property ownership at that time and, indirectly, useful farming information.

The boundaries of owned or tenanted property were drawn on a 25" O.S. map and its details recorded in a 'Field Book' along with the valuation. Apart from giving a description of the farm house, it listed the outbuildings stating their use and condition. Thus the eight bedroomed Holly Farm with its two sitting rooms and dairy had, as outbuildings, two cowsheds, which together could accommodate 23 cows, a stable for three horses, a pigsty and other buildings described as being in fair or poor condition. The whole, including its 100 acres, was valued at £2411.

Cumulatively the Field Book entries describe a parish of grass fields supporting dairy farms.

The other three surveys have a more direct relevance to farming. Land use surveys were conducted in the thirties and in the sixties. War time needs prompted the National Farm Survey 1941-1943. Of these only the pre-war Land Utilisation Survey was published in full in the form of reports and maps at the 1" scale. The data collected from the war time survey have only recently (1992) been available for public scrutiny and printed maps for the Second Land Utilisation Survey are limited to a few counties not including Nottinghamshire.

Holly Farm

The Land Utilisation Survey report for the county published in 1944 places Keyworth in the South Notts Wolds Grazing Region, thus summarising the influence of location, the heavy soil derived from the Mercia Mudstone and boulder clay, and of the topography on the farming in this part of the county. In common with neighbouring parishes Keyworth's farms had a high proportion of permanent grassland.

Milk production was important and during the thirties at least five Keyworth farms supplied milk to one or other of Nottingham's principal dairies, Nottingham Co-operative Society and Nottingham Dairy Ltd.

The 1942 survey provided information on a variety of matters not normally covered in the annual collection of agricultural statistics. It recorded the extent to which electric light and power was available for both domestic and farming purposes. Five farms were without electricity at all, whilst a similar number had lighting and power for both farm and domestic use. The other 14 farms had electricity mainly for the home. It was noted whether water was supplied to the farm and fields by pipe, well, roof or stream. On the questionnaires for Keyworth the inspector added 'ponds' to the list of water sources. The survey sought to determine the availability of powered machinery and the number of tractors on the farms. Only one of Keyworth's farms had a tractor, but there were 41 horses, about half of which were used for agricultural purposes.

Controversially, the quality of farm management was assessed as being:

well managed (A), fairly managed (B), or badly managed (C). Although none of Keyworth's 24 farms was described as being badly managed only four rated the A classification. In this respect the standard was far below the national average, in which 58% of farms were assessed as being well managed.

One of the aims of the survey was to delineate farm boundaries. In south Nottinghamshire the 6" OS maps were used for this purpose. When compared with the maps of the earlier survey they reveal changes over a 30-year period enabling one to enlarge on the comparisons made using the annual agricultural statistics. Thus the reduction in the number of farms did not necessarily mean a physical consolidation of the holdings. For example, by 1942, Frederick W. Howick, tenant of Holme Farm, had replaced the three tenants who had farmed the same land in 1914. However, it was still in four separate parcels just as at the earlier date. On the other hand, the land on Wolds Lane farmed by Samuel Armstrong was a consolidation of land which in 1914 was divided between two tenants. But the overall impression remains one of persisting fragmentation and only limited consolidation.

However, one of the legacies of pre-enclosure times has not persisted. A village street which once gave access to nigh on a dozen farms can boast but one.

Valuable and interesting as they are, statistics and surveys can only hint at the nature of farming life. This has to be told by those who worked on the farm and whose lives were shaped by its demands. Some of their reminiscences complete this chapter.

'There was some as could afford only three farthings worth'
Memories of Tom Oldham, born 1 April 1903

Tom's earliest memories were of his grandad who lived in Rose Cottage on Selby Lane. This he rented from the rector along with 20 acres of grass land on which he kept 12 milking cows, mostly Lincoln Reds. About 1910, Grandad bought 44 acres of land from the former Bunny Estate, of which 12 were ploughed. A further 11 acres, known as the Water Willows, were acquired when the rector, Henry Ling, sold the church land in 1918.

Tom can remember that before going to school he used to deliver milk in Keyworth and Stanton on his bike. He carried a bucket and pint and half pint measures. The cost was 1½d per pint, but some could only afford ¾d worth.

In the summer he would 'tent' [tend?] the cows on the roadside verge which was let annually for this purpose. In the winter the cows were inside; one of his tasks then was to help take the cows each morning to the Stockwell Pump. At night he would assist in watering by bucket from the farm's well.

By the age of 12, during the First World War, he was helping with the harvest at the family farm and on neighbouring farms.

He left school at 13, the leaving age, to work on the farm and can remember using a flail for the first and only time to thresh beans for cattle feed. He stayed only a few months as getting up turnips covered in snow and sharp frost didn't seem a fair task, even for this hardy lad.

'Mixed milk is egg-noggy'

Recollections of Les Sewell

Les Sewell of Welldale Farm on the Bunny to East Leake road, spent his early childhood in Keyworth. His grandfather, William Sewell, is shown in an old photograph controlling one of the bulls which served the village herds. The bulls, usually Lincoln Reds, were bought at Lincoln Market, brought by train to Plumtree Station and driven to the farm from there.

Les recalls the bull being taken daily to the square for its drink. The bulls were usually docile, but he does remember one which pinned him against the wall and was only shifted when his brother stuck a pitchfork into the beast's rear!

One of his abiding memories is of old farmer Cheatle carrying his milk in yoked buckets, trudging flat-footed from his farm opposite Hodgett's smithy to the Sewells' farm. Here, Grandma Sewell, during the eight warmest months

A tractor of the 1930s

Threshing at Shaw's Farm. Reproduced with the permission of Nottinghamshire County Council Library Service, Local Studies Section.

of the year, made Stilton and Colwick Cheese using milk from six local farms. The mixing of milk for this purpose was acceptable, but the Misses Carter of Factory Yard described such milk as 'egg-noggy' and insisted that their supplies came from one cow only!

'Threshing — the most exciting job on the farm'

Tom Branson's recollections of the twenties and thirties

In the early 1920s, Tom Branson lived at Manor Farm with his uncles, the Beswick brothers. This 61 acre farm lay mainly between Bunny and Debdale Lanes and was large by comparison with others in the parish. Most farms were smaller and generally farther spread which had considerable implications for machinery. Shaw's (later Henry Plowright's) farm and Pickard's farm were compact, but Harry Holmes' fields were scattered from Selby Lane to the far side of Rancliffe Wood. George Cutts, too, had a farm with fields near the present industrial site and others to the east of Nottingham Road.

The first ever tractor in Keyworth was bought by the Beswick brothers in 1922. Tom remembers as a child sitting on its tank and riding between Bunny and Keyworth.

Most farms had only one, two or three workers for most of the year but more were needed for harvesting and threshing. On the smaller farms casual labour was often provided in the evening by men from other farms after milking.

Haymaking and harvesting were two of the great events in the agricul-

Agricultural scene, Lings Lane

tural year. In haymaking, two horses were used for pulling the machine to cut the swatches which were 'tedded into windrows'. The hay was transported to the stockyard by wagon. When harvesting, the binder was pulled by two to four horses and the stooked sheaves of corn taken to the yard to await the arrival of the threshing machine some time between October and the following April.

For sheer dramatics the arrival of the threshing machine took some beating. Tom described threshing as the most exciting job on the farm, even if it was the dirtiest. It was done by contractors. The two great characters in the 20s and 30s were Tommy Taylor, and later, J.D. (Dixie) Ball. Taylor's home base was next to The Salutation from where his driver, Ernie Brain, would take the threshing machine from farm to farm. Dixie Ball originally operated from the Keepers' Cottages in Bunny but later moved to Hebb's Stack Yard (Middletons). Threshing was generally a job for seven to nine workers who between them operated the traction engine, controlled the drum to cut the binder twine, got the sheaves from stack to drum and carried the sacks of grain, which could weigh up to two hundredweight, up the steps into the granary. The threshing machine could at the same time operate an additional piece of ancillary equipment. This might be, for example, a chaff cutter or an elevator.

The grain was usually graded into three commercial qualities with a fourth group of 'tailings' given to the farmer's wife for her poultry. She was a vital member of the threshing team, for she provided the regular mugs of steaming tea, an antidote to the large volumes of choking dust generated by the threshing machines. The steam-driven traction engine was fuelled with coal. Traditionally, it was the farmer's responsibility to provide this, not only for his own task, but enough to see the threshing 'train' to its next venue. Clifton Colliery was the usual source.

Unlike at Bunny, where most farms grew potatoes and where children were given a fortnight off school to lift them, only a few acres were devoted to this crop in Keyworth. Manor Farm was the only one to produce potatoes commercially.

Tom remembers the cheesemaking in the village. He relates how the Woods produced Stilton at Upper Broughton and later at Keyworth. The first consignment of their Keyworth Stilton was rejected by Skinner and Rook - the up-market grocers in Nottingham - as being inedible. When tried back in Keyworth it was reported as being more suitable for the soling of boots! Nothing more has been heard of this Keyworth Stilton.

On the other hand Colwick Cheese continued to be made by the Davills using the surplus milk produced during the summer months. Davill's Colwick Cheese, shaped like an upside down flan, was priced according to diameter, 6" and 8" cheeses costing 6d and 9d respectively. At the time a farm labourer's wage was 35s a week.

Chapter 8

Pipes and Wires

During the last hundred years public services have developed beyond measure. Changes appeared in both extent and scale. In the late nineteenth century Keyworth's needs were for a reliable clean water supply and the chance to dispose of modest quantities of sewage and refuse.

The first half of the twentieth century saw telegraph services augmented with a modest spread of telephones, the introduction of gas and electricity and improvements in water supply and sewage disposal.

Road maintenance, refuse disposal and public cleansing were once locally based and labour-intensive. Today they are mechanised and are organised at Borough Council level.

These developments accelerated sharply when Keyworth began to expand from 1960 onwards as a commuter settlement.

Water Supply

At the end of the nineteenth century the village depended on wells and pumps for local supply. Many were shared, including the village pump east of the Church — which was padlocked at times of drought when the flow began to fail! Some sources on Bunny Lane were reported as polluted owing to the presence of magnesium sulphate leaked out of the local strata.

Early in the 1900s some households enjoyed local deliveries of tanker water. It is thought that some dwellings were connected to water pipe supplies by 1920.

The first proper supply was derived from a borehole into the bunter pebble beds near Oxton. This fed a local reservoir before being piped to the reservoir on Wilford Hill at a height of about 260 feet above sea level. Nottingham Corporation Water Department then laid a nine inch main via the Old Coach Road, Landmere Lane and along the A606 to serve Tollerton and Plumtree.

This was extended to the Normanton Booster (beside Plumtree station bridge), where an electric pump moved water along a nine inch pipe under pressure to Stanton Water Tower (on Brown's Lane) around 1928. This storage provided capacity and pressure to serve Keyworth and some adjacent settlements. By 1962 demands were increasing and a second booster pump was installed on the Normanton site.

The construction of large new reservoir capacity at Church Wilne enabled the water undertaking (now the Severn Trent Water Authority) to pump water up to Strelley Reservoir at a height of over 300 feet. This, when connected into local mains, provides a pressure head for Keyworth.

During 1975–76 the water authority constructed a south area trunk main which ran via Beeston, Clifton, Ruddington and Plumtree to Willow Brook. Here the new 400 millimetre pipe linked into the existing nine inch village supply pipes. This rendered the Normanton boosters and the Stanton Tower redundant. The former buildings were sold off and the tower was demolished.

Nowadays demand is approaching the limits of capacity, and a small in-line booster pump has been installed at the west end of Browns Lane to improve flow to Stanton and Hickling.

The original village mains were cast iron and postwar housing was largely served by ductile iron mains. Modern piping (and some replacement mains) are laid with MDPE (Medium Density Polyethylene) blue plastic pipes.

The change in source from borehole to river supplies caused minor problems in Keyworth around 1980. A combination of circumstances led to many dwellings suffering from pin-hole leaks developing in copper water service pipes, but this trouble has now all but vanished.

Sewage Disposal

The volume of sewage is largely dependent on the supply of water in a locality. At the end of the last century modest supplies were drawn from wells and disposal usually went into local watercourses or finished up in earth closets and cesspits. Since those days water supply has developed and public usage has grown apace. After the Second World War the average inhabitant used about fifteen gallons daily. By 1990 the usage had risen to almost thirty gallons per head, plus industrial and commercial use. Washing machines, dishwashers and lavish bathrooms have contributed to this change.

During the early years of this century sewers were laid in the main and residential streets of Keyworth. Many were 'combined', taking foul and some stormwater flows. These flows ran by gravity to sewer dykes, at which points primitive retention or treatment plants were built, and from which watery effluent overflowed into local watercourses. Main sewers led towards the site of the present treatment works south of Bunny Lane, south from Lings Lane, down Debdale Lane and along Willow Brook.

These provided a measure of disposal for Keyworth. Isolated dwellings were served by cesspits. A collection service developed whereby closet waste was collected in a horse-drawn tumbril tanker.

From 1960 onwards Keyworth grew in population and sewage works were installed to cope with increasing flow. A modern treatment plant was constructed south of Bunny Lane and part of Keyworth's outflow gravitated there. The remainder flowed to pumping stations at the foot of Nicker Hill and at the end of Debdale Lane, from where flow was pumped to higher levels to gravitate to the works.

In early years works were the responsibility of parish and rural district councils. After the Second World War the Trent River Board pressed for better standards of discharge. From 1974 onwards powers passed to the Severn-Trent Water Authority, with Rushcliffe Borough Council acting as agents.

The growth in development and population, and the need to replace outdated sewers, pumping equipment and other plant has led to some major works in Keyworth, especially during 1979 and 1987. Currently Severn Trent Water Authority is carrying out a major computer-based study of sewage facilities so that future investment can be planned to best advantage.

Keyworth is fortunate in its siting, with stormwater flow and foul sewage normally running smoothly towards watercourses and/or treatment plants.

Gas Supply

Gas works in Nottingham were built by the Gas, Light and Coke Company during the nineteenth century, and later operations were taken over by Nottingham Corporation. From 1930 onwards supplies were extended from Edwalton towards Tollerton, Plumtree and Keyworth. In addition to domestic use, some street gas lamps served the village streets. The East Midlands Gas Board then took over services.

Demand grew and in 1961 a new governor was installed at the bottom of Nicker Hill to cope with increased pressures. Keyworth continued to expand and in 1968 supplies were augmented by a new gas main which was laid from Ruddington across country to link in via a gas pressure governor kiosk at the west end of Debdale Lane.

Around 1970 the source of supply changed from town gas manufactured from coal to that of North Sea Gas. This major undertaking met the rising demand in Keyworth, firstly because the natural gas had a calorific value twice that of old gas and secondly because it was fed at eight inches water gauge pressure instead of four inches — in effect quadrupling the supply capacity.

The sophisticated operation to convert to North Sea Gas was carried out with quiet efficiency. Not only did gas governor kiosks and gas mains require alterations, but all domestic and commercial appliances had to be modified to burn the new, hotter gas. Quite a nine days' wonder at the time, but carried out by the Gas Board and its contractors with considerable success!

New services and mains are now laid in yellow plastic piping. New meters appeared in all premises.

Electricity Supply

Electricity distribution in Nottingham City was a self-contained business. Surrounding rural areas had to wait until the late twenties before other sources of supply became available.

The Derby and Nottinghamshire Power Company built a station at Spondon and shortly afterwards laid an 11,000 volts line eastwards to reach the cement factory at Barnstone. This overhead line passed south of Keyworth and a spur was laid to bring power into the village at 240 volts. A number of local farms also received a supply via their own small transformers in return for giving wayleave to the overhead line. Since those days a steady extension of supply and upgrading of lines has continued. Many lines began as overhead supplies but were later put underground as urban development grew.

The policy of the Power Company was to establish ring feeds within their territory and to supply in bulk to any local authority able to provide for distribution. The company was an associate of the old MIDESCO (Midlands Electric Supply Company) which co-ordinated supply in the midlands between the wars. To supplement supply the company began the construction of the first generating plant at Staythorpe, just before nationalisation. Thereafter the EMEB (East Midlands Electricity Board) dealt with distribution of supply received from the National Grid.

The supply to Keyworth operated from 1928. A substation was established at Selby Lane, with an overhead line carrying power northward to another substation at Nicker Hill. Later, this substation was additionally fed from a high voltage line feeding from the direction of Clipston Wolds. In 1936 wayleaves to protect the route of lines were purchased on either side of Selby Lane. Later still these lines were upgraded to 33,000 volts and by 1965 a link was established on double 'H' wooden poles carrying two circuits from the developing major substation northwest of Willoughby-on-the-Wolds. Currently this supply operates at 132,000 volts with supply transformed down to serve Keyworth.

From 1960 onwards urban development grew apace in Keyworth and numerous local substations were built to provide domestic supplies. The cables for these were laid underground, as was the service leading to Plumtree.

The major visual feature on the local skyline is now the 400,000 volts supergrid line, whose pylons stride from Ratcliffe-on-Soar Power Station to Staythorpe Power Station, passing between Keyworth and Plumtree.

Refuse Collection and Public Cleansing

A century ago the very rural settlement of Keyworth had no refuse collection system. Domestic waste was burnt on coal fires, disposed of with midden emptyings, or — occasionally — tipped in local hollows.

By the 1930s refuse was collected by the rural district council using side-loading lorries which removed waste weekly and disposed of it into old quarries or other local voids.

The growth of population saw the introduction of larger and more sophisticated vehicles which had rear-loading, crusher type bodies. These reduced dust and disturbance and enabled far more material to be taken to each load. The latter was an important factor, for with the commissioning of the Meadow Lane refuse incinerator by the Nottingham City Council, most refuse collected in the greater Nottingham area was dealt with there. The heat so generated was used to serve central area district heating schemes. Local authorities had an assured disposal point.

From 1974 onwards the re-organisation of local government caused disposal to pass to the County Councils as a responsibility, with district Councils charged with the task of refuse collection.

Refuse quantities continued to grow with the advent of domestic central heating. Rushcliffe Borough Council countered this by introducing larger and more efficient collection vehicles, some with three axles. Experiments were made in separate collection of waste paper in trailers towed by collection vehicles but the variation in disposal prices and safety requirements for operations led to the abandonment of trailers.

The Borough Council turned to the use of black plastic refuse sacks by the 1980s as a way of increasing output of its workers and to reduce dust and pollution during loading operations.

The desirability of re-using waste materials led to the public co-operating with the local authority when the latter established bottle banks for glass waste. Keyworth has three (white, green and brown glass) established in the car park off Bunny Lane. This facility is heavily used.

Street cleansing and refuse collection has been privatised since 1992 and the Borough's vehicles now include mechanised street and footpath sweepers as well as small versions of refuse collection trucks which deal with litter bins and the special needs of local shopping centres.

Highways

During the latter years of the nineteenth century the village streets of Keyworth were roughly metalled and kept in fair repair by a highway authority which split its duties between County Council and Parish Council.

By the end of the First World War the main roads were given tarmac surfaces by the County Council and this work continued over minor roads which linked villages. Some street lighting by gas appeared in the village centre.

After the Second World War a number of streets in Keyworth were only roughly metalled and had not been adopted as public highways. Once Keyworth began to grow as a commuter settlement, new residential streets were built to proper specifications and then formally adopted by the County

Council as highway authority. This work eventually extended over most unadopted streets as well.

Highway maintenance work was to some extent delegated to Bingham Rural District whilst the Parish Council saw to street lighting.

The major reorganisation of local government in 1974 saw the formation of the larger Rushcliffe Borough Council, which undertook increasing responsibility in minor street works, public cleansing and gully emptying, with such duties moving solely to the Borough Council in 1992.

Today the following roads are graded as category C highways within Keyworth:

C80   Nottingham Road
C101 Selby Lane
C20   Nicker Hill and the route to Plumtree
C125 Willow Brook

This categorisation reflects the growth of traffic within Keyworth, its use by bus services and the need to take account of the main road framework serving the built-up area. Maintenance costs for these and other minor roads is the responsibility of the County Council.

Telegraphy

From the early 1880s Plumtree Railway Station enjoyed telegraph facilities. Subsequently Plumtree Post Office operated a telegram service, firstly by telegraph and later by telephone. The area served stretched from Tollerton Railway Bridge to Widmerpool and Keyworth with telegrams dispatched by hand from the post office: telegram services were closed down in the 1970s.

Early in the twentieth century telephone subscribers were connected to a manual exchange based in Plumtree post office. This also incorporated an attended call service. By 1929 increased use resulted in the exchange being transferred to premises in Rose Grove, where manual equipment served the Plumtree, Normanton and Keyworth localities until 1958. By this time subscribers exceeded 500 and numbers were rising rapidly.

The solution was the construction of an automatic exchange in Plumtree and this was the subject of extensions in later years to meet ever-rising demand. Improvements in exchange equipment and the need to simplify services led to the Plumtree exchange being subsumed into the Nottingham system in 1990 with the consequent disappearance of Plumtree as an exchange name. The ever-increasing demand for telephone line capacity has led to the introduction of revised and slightly larger telephone numbers during the latter part of 1994.

Chapter 9

'Tickets Please'

During the past hundred years Keyworth and surrounding villages have been served by various modes of transport for the movement of people and goods. Most of the journeys have been between Keyworth and Nottingham.

The railway has played an important part in the development of transport in the area. The Midland Railway opened up in 1880 for business between Nottingham and Melton Mowbray. The local station was 'Plumtree and Keyworth' and sited in the village of Plumtree, to the north of Keyworth. George Thomas Bursnell, who began his duties in 1881, was the first stationmaster. The passenger business gradually grew in numbers as the railway became an important part of the local transport system between Plumtree and Nottingham. Eventually, with the increased competition from road transport and other factors, Plumtree station was closed to passenger traffic in 1949.

John Ingamells, who was the stationmaster during the 1950s, did attempt to reopen the station to passenger traffic as the number of commuters requiring transport to Nottingham increased. Although some holiday excursions were arranged in an attempt to maintain passenger traffic, the growth of private motoring and competitively priced bus travel meant that Plumtree station remained closed to regular services.

Also sited at Plumtree was a freight depot. It handled mainly cattle feed, coal and the brick and concrete products from Baldwins of Bunny. Silcocks had a distribution centre for cattle feed at the depot and for 30 years prior to the Second World War Tom Bexon operated as a coal merchant. With the changing patterns in the movement of goods and the increase in road transport, Fred Saunders, the last stationmaster, finally saw the freight depot close down in 1965. Although the passenger service and goods yard activities had ceased, the railway line was still used until Dr

Plumtree and Keyworth Station

Beeching finally closed it in the 1960s. Meanwhile a trolleybus preservation society used the goods yard for a number of years. Even today part of the track is used as a test line for the development of new rolling stock.

Plumtree station, which still stands, has served the local residents for many decades. In fact it still does, as the excellent meals served by Perkins Bar Bistro have banished all memories of railway sandwiches!

From railways to something a little smaller: was the bicycle a Keyworth invention? An undated newspaper article by H.J. Chilton reads as follows:

'At some unspecified date probably in the 1870s, Matthew Hodgett brought Keyworth into the limelight by constructing a primitive bicycle. The claim has been made with what justification is unknown, that he was actually the inventor of the machine which revolutionised our habits.

'This early model had iron tyres and the component parts were ingeniously integrated by a broad flat iron spring. This formed a connecting link with the front and back wheels and the saddle was attached to it.

'This remarkable machine announced its oncoming by the menacing rattle of its iron wheels on the rough roads and a bell was quite unnecessary.

'It is regretted to report that this historic bicycle ended its days on a scrap heap and not in its rightful place, a museum.'

Maybe Keyworth does not have this claim to fame after all.

In 1979 the late Deborah Tomlinson, a Keyworth resident, recalled that when she was a child in the late nineteenth century, cycles were very scarce. She could only remember three in Keyworth. Her father owned one, Claud Pike the second, and she could not recollect the third owner.

How did these early cyclists find the road conditions? There were two men responsible for repairing the roads (one for the north side of Keyworth and one for the south side). The stones for the repair work were fetched principally from the Stonepits at North Lodge Farm, Widmerpool. At a later date the stone was brought to the village via Plumtree Station and into Keyworth by horse and cart. The stones were tipped into the ruts and holes and then other traffic (i.e. other carts) had to work these stones down over a period into some sort of surface.

In the 1890s passengers and goods were moved to and from Keyworth by carriers using horse-drawn waggons. George Linney from Upper Broughton came through Keyworth three days a week en route to Nottingham. John Holmes of Keyworth was a local carrier with his horse-drawn covered vehicle. He transported passengers and goods to Nottingham twice a week, on Wednesdays and Saturdays. He frequently made the trip between Keyworth and the station in Plumtree. Six passengers could ride inside his wagonette and the goods travelled on the roof. George Barnett from Willoughby served Keyworth whilst travelling to Nottingham. Normanton also had a carrier, Sarah Clarke, who seems only to have travelled to Nottingham on a Saturday.

Prior to the railway's opening, coal was transported from Clifton Colliery to Keyworth by horse and cart. It was a whole day's journey. As most houses had no back door, the coal was tipped on the paths and roads at the front door of the house. The occupier then had to move the coal indoors. Joseph Pike and Edward Westerday were coal merchants and distributed coal using horse-drawn drays.

The early years of this century saw more competition for the transportation of goods and people. Henry Pears from Upper Broughton came through Keyworth and Plumtree on his way to Nottingham. Henry Lacey ran a horse-drawn cab service between Keyworth and Plumtree Station. The population of Keyworth had now increased to around 800, providing more work for the carriers in the area. Frank Cantrill was the local police officer, presumably with fewer traffic problems to deal with than his successors.

Samuel Wright lived in the old blacksmith's premises at the corner of Cedar Drive and Main Street. He moved to Blind Lane (now Commercial Road) where he developed a hardware shop and delivery service. He used a wagonette for his deliveries. Around the period of the First World War he had developed the service in competition with John Holmes and Henry Lacey. The carrier service would take passengers from Keyworth to Nottingham. In addition Samuel Wright would carry golfers from Plumtree Station to the nine hole golf course at Stanton on the Wolds for 3d each, returning them to the Griffin public house at Plumtree for an evening beer. The wagonette had large wheels at the rear, smaller ones at the front, and was suspended by

Harry Davinson, carrier and coal merchant, seen here with his coal cart at New Corner.

leather straps. It held six people and was drawn by a single horse. Sam's business expanded with trade deliveries and passenger services to such an extent that he had four horses in the stables on Blind Lane.

George Wright, one of Sam's eleven children, borrowed 50s 0d to buy stock and started repairing cycles in a shed on Selby Lane. However after six months the First World War had broken out and he was posted to France. On his return from the war in 1919, George started to buy cars, used them as taxis for awhile, then dismantled the vehicles and sold the parts as spares. He was now also selling petrol in tins at 10d a gallon with total weekly sales for Keyworth being around 16 gallons. In the mid-1920s George bought his second bus. It was a Morris Gem and had seats which faced each other along the length of the bus. In 1926 he had an advertisement in *The Advertiser* (Saturday, 24 April 1926). It read 'Cycle and Motor Cycle Agent. Sole District Agent for Raleigh. Repairs a Speciality. Petrol, Oil, Tyres and Accessories. Cars for Hire. Phone: Y6 Keyworth (Ruddington Exchange).'

In the same paper appeared advertisements for 'ELDING'S OWN BUS. ALL ALONE ON HIS OWN AND LONG MAY YOUR LUMS REEK'. Then followed his timetable from Keyworth to Nottingham (Collin Street). There were about nine trips a day during the week and eleven journeys on a Saturday. The first bus left Keyworth at 7.15 a.m. — the last bus from Nottingham on a Saturday was 10.30 p.m. There were just five journeys to Nottingham on a Sunday. A third advertisement was for 'HECTOR TOMLINSON, 5

DEBDALE LANE, KEYWORTH, CARRIER, WEDNESDAY AND SATUR-
DAYS' (Between several local villages) 'GOODS OF ANY DESCRIPTION
REMOVED. INQUIRIES INVITED. ESTIMATES FREE. PERSONAL ATTEN-
TION. REASONABLE CHARGES'

By 1922 the local constable was Harry Moorhouse, who now had to over-
see a population of over 1000. With the increasing population more passenger carrying vehicles and carriers were appearing on the streets of Keyworth.

In the mid twenties Herbert Mills began transporting milk. Over the years
he developed a sizeable business as a haulage contractor. Harry Davinson
delivered coal from Plumtree station to Keyworth households, using a horse-
drawn cart. Harry was known on several occasions to time his collection of
coal at the station with the arrival of two churns of ice cream on the passenger train. These he then carried to the grocer's shop on Debdale Lane to the
awaiting queue. When Harry began to use vehicles he kept them in immacu-
late condition. Stan Price remembers him stopping his lorry and crawling
underneath to wipe clean the underside of the vehicle to remove the dust
and dirt accumulated from driving on unmade roads. The business was eventually passed over to his son George, who is still serving the community.
George Davis, another well known coal merchant, began his deliveries in
1928 and continued into the 1940s. Tommy Hebb also got his hands dirty
delivering coal from the station and tipping it on the street outside his cus-
tomer's house. It then had to be carried through or barrowed to the rear of
the house. Yet another local carrier was Alan Tomlinson, who began transporting goods in 1927.

The largest growth was in passenger transport. Arthur Ellis was one of
the first to introduce a bus into Keyworth. He was based on Bunny Lane.
Two stories emerge regarding his buses. He had a Vulcan coach which unfortunately caught fire near the Toll Bar (between Tollerton and Edwalton).
The coach was completely burnt out and it is believed that it was not in-
sured. On another occasion a certain Tommy Taylor (rather the worse for
alcohol) fired a gun through the coach roof.

Arthur Howe created the 'Comfy' Bus Service. He was living in Plumtree
Park when he bought his first bus, which he used to keep in a large wooden
garage at his home. The bus service ran from Keyworth to Nottingham. While
Arthur was driving, his wife was collecting the fares. On most occasions
when returning from Nottingham, Arthur would take his passengers to their
own doorsteps. Service with a smile!

Barnetts from Widmerpool had an old coach which had bench seats down
either side and seated about 12 passengers. Holbrook and Elding Ltd of
Bunny Lane was another company travelling between Keyworth and Nottingham. They ran more than a dozen journeys each weekday. The single
fare according to their advertisements was 6d, return 1s 0d and 'Parties were
also catered for — telephone 62Y1 Ruddington'. Jimmy Atkins from Beeston
ran a service from Keyworth to Nottingham. He had about four red buses in
his business. Ideal Buses, based in Ruddington, also served Keyworth for a
time.

Arthur Howes, one of the early bus operators, with his wife, who was the conductress.

The competition for passengers became fierce. Each operator would try to race the opposition to the next bus stop in order to gain more passengers. The situation arose whereby when passengers boarded a bus at Keyworth heading for Nottingham, the fare would not be collected until reaching Plumtree. If there were few passengers on the bus and there were no further passengers boarding at Plumtree, everyone was turned off the bus to await the following service. It was not worth taking a few passengers all the way to Nottingham. The empty bus would return to Keyworth.

Eventually the smaller bus companies were consolidated into larger fleets. Jimmy Atkins sold out to Bartons Transport Ltd of Chilwell. Arthur Howe's buses also ended up under the control of Bartons when Mrs Howe sold out in 1932. The blue buses from the Ideal Bus Co. from Ruddington, after various take-overs, also ended up under Bartons' control.

There were various route changes between Bartons and Midland Red Buses, leaving Bartons the only bus company serving Keyworth. Some of their earlier buses used on the local routes were called Gliders and produced a very distinctive noise with the whine from the rear axle.

CIVILITY AND SERVICE

As the village grew, some of the local traders ran their own vehicles. Fred Disney, who started his local bakery business in 1910, used a pony and trap to deliver his products to Keyworth and Normanton. Vera Bishop used to earn 6d a week from Mr Disney by holding his horse, which had a habit of bolting! Cyril Disney, who followed on, had a Model T Ford van before the Second World War. He unfortunately broke his wrist on several occasions when trying to start the vehicle with the crank handle. The Co-op store in the village had a horse-drawn delivery van, superseded by a small motor van. This was eventually replaced with a larger vehicle. Across the rear doors it read 'Nottinghamshire Co-op — 55000 members. Are You One of Them?'. Ken Bishop worked with Les Bloor delivering groceries to a large round covering many of the local villages.

In the early days there were two other necessary services requiring transport. Before the installation of running water, Bob Smith the 'night soil man' used to empty the tubs from the toilets. The contents helped to fertilize some of the local crops! The advertisement for the other essential service read, 'R. Rimmer, Mill Yard, Keyworth. Reasonable charges. Distance no object. Personal Attention'. He was located by the Windmill on Selby Lane, and was of course the local funeral director offering that final journey!

Keyworth has grown considerably during the last three decades. Private motoring has also grown to enormous proportions. During 1988 parking restrictions were introduced in the centre of the village and on some of the main roads. There is an occasional visit from a traffic warden.

The number of haulage contractors in the village has diminished mainly because they have needed to move out to obtain larger premises. In the 1960s Herbert Mills sold his haulage business to Garrett and Hemphrey, who continued to operatefrom Keyworth for a time. In 1977 they moved to Nottingham for greater opportunities. Eric Elliott moved his haulage business from Plumtree to Keyworth in the 1970s, but owing to the expansion of his business he had to leave Keyworth in 1993 for larger premises in Gotham.

In the 1930s you could ring Plumtree 34 for George Wright's taxi service. More recently Mellors Taxis served the village from 1970 to 1988 and we now have Grosvenor Taxis.

It was during the late 1980s that the regulations controlling which bus operators could use which routes were eased. Deregulation brought several new bus companies into Keyworth searching for more profitable routes. In some cases the bus fare to Nottingham was halved from £1 to 50p. We also saw the same situation which occurred fifty years ago — too many buses for the number of passengers. Some companies put on additional buses to put pressure on the competing operators. Once again buses were speeding to Nottingham, attempting to get to the next stop before the opposition.

Bartons were the main bus operators to the village for several decades. But Malcolm Gagg from Bunny came on the scene with cut price fares and very friendly staff. On one occasion it is recalled where the driver stopped at a phone box to allow the passenger to telephone ahead to see if Aunty Flo was at home before she continued her journey! On another occasion, a regular passenger, who travelled to Ruddington to visit her elderly mother quite

82

George Wright driving a 1927 Renault, with his wife Laura. George (junior) standing, Bernard in the centre and Charles on the right. Note Selby Lane windmill in the background. Reproduced by courtesy of Stephen Wright.

frequently, had her American sister staying in Keyworth. You should have seen her expression when a Gaggs driver pulled up in his bus, opened the door and yelled, 'How's your mother today?' before continuing his journey. 'I don't believe it. A bus driver stops his bus to ask how Mother is. That wouldn't happen back home!' It certainly was service with a smile. Unfortunately Malcolm Gagg could not compete with the big bus companies on the regular bus routes. Today he has school contracts and private hire, plus two trips to Eastern Europe under his belt!

During the deregulation we saw Nottingham City Transport, Midland Fox, Pathfinder and other bus operators plying for business in Keyworth. Today Bartons and Pathfinder of Newark offer the regular bus services.

Meanwhile our own local bus operator was gradually expanding. Much has happened since George Wright began repairing cycles in a hut on Selby Lane. Steven Wright now has a fleet of private hire coaches looking after school contracts and private outings all over the UK. In addition, the garage will service and repair your vehicle and you can be refuelled with a smile. Unfortunately the price of petrol has increased from ten pence a gallon (pre-decimal coinage) to over £2!

One final thought in this journey through a hundred years of local transport history: there is a service, reviving a form of transport invented in the eighteenth century, which will take you on a journey, hopefully of delight, destination unknown!

'All aboard for lift off with Celebration Balloon Flights, Keyworth 1994'.

Chapter 10

The Impact of the First and Second World Wars

The First World War disturbed rural communities on an unprecedented scale. In 1914 the local Territorials were mobilised for war. Volunteers followed them and as the war progressed most able-bodied young men were conscripted to service.

Casualties were heavy and the Parish Church war memorial records the names of 27 men. Of these ten served in the Sherwood Foresters and two in the South Notts Hussars. The remainder were listed from other units, as follows:

1	Grenadier Guardsman
2	Royal Artillery
1	East Lancashire Regt.
1	South Lancashire Regt.
1	North Lancashire Regt.
3	Kings Royal Rifles
1	Royal West Kent Regt.
1	Royal Sussex Regt.
1	Royal Fusilier
2	Lincolnshire Regt.
1	Royal Marine

The grouping of names in Lancashire and South-East regiments may have arisen from the regrouping of units following heavy losses towards the end of the war, with men moved into other regiments. Of those listed, one was a sergeant and two were corporals. These ranks may reflect a rural population with few technicians and little grammar school opportunity.

The Second World War brought danger and fighting services' bases into the local rural scene. Once again the local Territorials went off to war but in a different guise. Local infantry battalions climbed into trucks and the South Notts Hussars abandoned their horses and functioned as an artillery regiment. Voluntary service and conscription saw many young men move into the armed services.

Circumstances were very different in this war. Wider education saw a much more varied spread of service duties for combatants, with all three armed services taking recruits from this once quiet rural area.

The Parish Church war memorial reflects this change. Losses included four Royal Air Force men, presumably of aircrew standard. Two were listed in the Leicestershire Regiment and one in the Royal Hampshire Regiment. One Royal Artilleryman was numbered, and one munitions worker. Fatal casualties were only one third those of the First World War from the Keyworth community.

The extent to which the armed services imposed a presence on the Keyworth locality during the Second World War was far greater than that in 1914–18. The arrival of service establishments in South Nottinghamshire generally affected Keyworth, which could no longer regard itself as a small, self-contained settlement. The flexibility and rapid changes brought by modern war meant that such establishments changed in duties and occupancy by varied units as the conflict progressed. Finally, it was remarkable that the many buildings and other traces of these developments mostly vanished within a decade or two of the end of hostilities.

Greater Nottingham was defended by an outlying ring of anti-aircraft sites: the nearest to Keyworth was a searchlight unit housed in a field on the north side of Widmerpool Road at mr 628 297. A brick building with asbestos roof (now stabling horses) and traces of an access track survive. Presumably this was a standard 90 cm AA light, manned for much of the war by ATS servicewomen in the Royal Artillery.

Other camp sites grew up in the locality furnished with lightly constructed brick buildings and Nissen huts. Bunny Hall grounds was home to soldiery, with some buildings south of Bunny Lane at the rear of Paradise Farm at mr 597 303. Tollerton Hall became a base for a bomb disposal unit of the Royal Engineers, who dealt with very dangerous items over the East Midlands. One especially tricky task was the clearance of hundreds of small 'butterfly' anti-personnel bombs, which brought Grimsby to a standstill for several weeks in 1943.

Tollerton airfield saw a variety of service squadrons come and go. Some were RAF and others were USAF. The latter, flush with money and Hollywood charm, upset the local social pattern by providing competition at dances held in the Plumtree Burnside Hall and elsewhere. Some fall in standards occurred, with the pilfering of cycles and so on. The airfield had its own ring of brick and concrete octagonal pillboxes for defence against airborne marauders. Towards the end of the War, American paratroopers were based at Wollaton Hall Park and on occasions carried out major ground exercises in the Stanton area.

There were other inward movements into the Keyworth area. At the beginning of hostilities many school children were evacuated from city areas to remove them from the danger of air raids. Keyworth received children from the Yarmouth area and from Sheffield. Reception households were paid 5s 0d per week billeting money per child. Some evacuees stayed for the duration, joining the roll of the village school and taking part in other local activities.

As hostilities progressed, other arrivals appeared on the Keyworth scene. Prisoners of war, both Italian and German, were accommodated in camps at Bunny and Tollerton. Hutted facilities were set up on market garden land and paddocks in the area now occupied by the Hollies estate north of Debdale Lane. These men were employed largely as agricultural workers in a regime much like today's open prisons. Most locals and prisoners were philosophical about internment and rubbed along with little friction. As the war progressed their regime slowly eased and from 1946 onwards repatriation took them away. Some POWs were valued agricultural workers and 'lived in' at farms where they served. Some acquaintances turned into friendships and correspondence developed later between farmers' families and repatriated POWs. The ability to judge prisoners as people rather than as enemies gave hope for the future.

Later in the war huge quantities of ammunition and war material were stored locally, partly to disperse explosives (to limit damage from bombing raids or accident) and partly to prepare for the needs of D-Day operations. Many fields and roadside verges around Keyworth accommodated hundreds of small corrugated iron semi-circular shelters which protected a wide variety of ordnance stores.

The Second World War saw virtually all able-bodied men and many younger women donning uniform for active service or part-time duties. Those not called to the colours served in the special constabulary, the auxiliary fire service (later the NFS), civil defence, ambulance service, coal mining (the

Auxiliary Fire Service with trailer pump. Left to right: Les Bloor, Tom Lomas, Alwyn Middleton, Bill Pike, Fred Swanborough.

Bevin Boys), local defence volunteers (later the Home Guard), the observer corps and the fire watchers. Women joined men in these duties, and staffed other invaluable services such as the Women's Land Army and the WVS as well.

Like regular forces, the voluntary and part-time services saw an ebb and flow of workload and priorities. Their duties and equipment changed to meet these needs. Whilst most part-timers were hard-working and enthusiastic volunteers, an element of conscription was employed to bolster numbers from the middle of the war onwards.

The voluntary forces played an essential part in home defence. Special Constabulary took over many police duties. The NFS manned many normal fire engines and staffed numerous trailer-drawn fire pumps in addition. All dealt with the many and widespread fires caused by incendiary bomb raids and often crews were employed well beyond their own 'patch' to meet emergencies in hard-pressed urban areas. Keyworth had a vehicle and trailer pump based near the square.

Civil Defence workers kept an eye on vital blackout regulations and gas precautions, checked air raid shelters, put out minor incendiary fires and coped with bomb damage and rescue work. St John's Ambulance Brigade and the British Red Cross helped in this work by driving ambulances, aiding stretcher bearers and in ancillary hospital duties. Any building of consequence had its quota of civilian firewatchers who 'lived in' nightly and with their own light firefighting equipment prevented many small incendiary fires becoming conflagrations.

The Memorial Gates which commemorate the fallen of the two world wars. Their restoration was made possible by a donation from the Sisters of Loreto.

The Observer Corps worked closely with the RAF and manned a network of observation posts across the kingdom. They recorded and tracked the passage of all aircraft (friendly and otherwise) overhead and any other matters visibly connected with the air by day and by night. Keyworth contributed observers to the Wymeswold post.

The Home Guard began as the Local Defence Volunteers, manning roadblocks with pitifully few weapons in the dark days after Dunkirk, and patrolling rural areas to spot paratroop and glider-borne intrusion. They soon moved to a formal basis as Home Guard battalions of the local county regiment and finished the war with weapons and equipment rather better than those of inter-war Territorial units. Once the immediate danger of invasion passed, their duties spread to guarding local features of value against sabotage or other attack. These included the Home Office radio station beside Brown's Lane at mr 635 305, and the Stanton Railway tunnel which carried vital coal and iron ore traffic to major industries. The Home Guard base was in old farm buildings on Brown's Lane. Most units were formed with a high proportion of men with grim experience of the First World War. Major Wheater and Captain Adams headed the local unit.

Keyworth had its share of wartime troubles. Several searchlights picked up one bomber which evaded lights by dropping its cargo to escape, with several bombs exploded between Nicker Hill and the Melton Road. A large parachute mine drifted off course to land (and detonate!) near Occupation

Lane at Wysall. Two bombs fell near Farnham Wood one summer and set undergrowth ablaze until the NFS arrived. A number of incendiary bombs scattered around Hickling also caused work for the NFS. One pompous man ignored a Home Guard checkpoint and drove through it, only to have his tyres shot out. Nobody drove past again without halting. The Observer Corps post spotted something mysterious drifting down from heaven in early morning sunshine; they tracked its fall and located it as a large map which had blown out of an RAF aircraft. The rightful owners were thunderstruck when it was returned to them shortly afterwards.

The First World War was a distant affair for Keyworth, with the community saddened by the long list of war dead. The Second World War imposed itself on the locality, with most members of the populace involved in some form of war service. Duties and fellowship drew everyone together in many respects, and brought a wider interest to what had been a placid rural community.

Chapter 11

Stanton and its Church

Stanton on the Wolds is a neighbouring parish of Keyworth. Here, on the low range of hills known as the Nottinghamshire Wolds, there existed in Saxon times a stone built farmstead although the land, consisting of glacial drift overlying impermeable clay, has never been considered desirable for farming. Following the Norman Conquest, the lordship of the manor of Stanton was held by the Clifton family, whose descendant Sir Mark Parsons (Baronet), before he died in 1812, lived alone in the old moated Manor House. It has been described as a mansion but, having fallen into disrepair, was converted into a redbrick farmhouse. By 1817, nearly all the land at Stanton had become part of the Widmerpool Hall Estate, which from 1870 was owned by Major G.C. Robertson, resident at the Hall.

The small ark-shaped church dedicated to All Saints dates from Norman times. Some of the fabric is fourteenth century. The chancel is of rubble masonry with tooled stone quoins. The nave built of undressed stones, probably collected from the fields, may be much later. At the beginning of the nineteenth century the building was in a deplorable condition. The historian Throsby described it as 'the most despicable place I ever beheld'. In 1889 Mrs Robertson, the squire's wife, paid £400 to restore it. Three years later, consequent on the death of the rector, the rector at Keyworth, the Rev Henry Ling, was granted his request that as the population of Stanton was only 107 the two livings should be held together, and then found that Stanton church could not pay its debts. A diocesan survey listed the church holdings as comprising the rectory, the adjoining farmhouse, four cottages together with 44 acres of glebe near the village and 80 acres, called 'Jerico', by the Fosse Way. The church sold this old land for £800 in 1894 and continued to sell off its glebe until the final sale in 1932 including the rectory and the field called Church Close, but preserving a right of way across it for access to the church.

The money received evidently did not solve the church's financial problems. The Nottingham Journal of 25 September 1950 reported that £1500 was needed for repairs. A successful appeal allowed restoration work to be carried out in 1951. In 1956 Cyril George Smith, a retired Indian army major, became a non-stipendiary vicar and stayed until 1971. The churchwardens, Philip Attewell and James Boucher, assisted in a period of parish activity. In 1973 Philip Attewell contrived with the architect, Vernon Royle, to add a vestry built in the same fashion as earlier stonework, using stones gathered from the fields by the children and farmers. A band of embroiderers led by Isobel Roadley of Laurel Farm provided sets of kneelers and seat runners. The crumbling fourteenth–century window was repaired in 1992. Tucked away in a field behind Laurel Farm, the church today is peaceful and attractive. A covenant scheme ensures that it has sufficient money to defray its costs.

At the end of the nineteenth century Stanton was a poor parish. In 1721 a former rector, the Rev Thomas Ousley, left in his will land at Gedling for the benefit of the poor at Stanton. In 1882 the land was sold and the money received was invested, the income being distributed to widows and needy half-yearly. The half-crown payment felt like gold to them. The Charity is still administered today and distributes £30 annually.

At the turn of the century most of the village population worked on the estate farms. There were three outlying farms: Stanton Lodge on Thurlby Lane, Bank Farm and Hill Farm on the east side of Melton Road. Also on the Melton Road were Stanton Odd Houses, four tied cottages occupied by estate workers. The other twenty or so households lived mainly around the church and manor.

William Page, a member of an old Stanton farming family, died in 1892 aged 79 years, having lived at the Manor House for much of the nineteenth century. He had farmed 510 acres, but as he grew older most of them were taken over by Joseph Page, who was the tenant at Page's Lodge, the farm to the north of the manor where the golf course is now. There was difficulty in finding another permanent tenant for Manor Farm. Eventually, on April Fool's Day 1902, newly married William and Elizabeth Bryans travelled by pony

Hill Farm,
Stanton - on - the - Wolds

and cart from Wysall to set up home in the Manor House. The farm was at first very small but increased over the years to about 120 acres. It was run by the whole family with little outside help. There was an orchard by the house containing three big walnut trees whose nuts they sold for pickling at 1s 0d per 100. Daughter Dorothy used to teach at Sunday School after helping with the milking. William Bryans represented Stanton on the Bingham Union and collected the half-yearly rates. In 1934 the Manor House, being very damp and in a poor state, was replaced by a new farmhouse at the corner of Browns Lane and Stanton Lane. The ground floor of the Old Manor House and also the farm buildings have now been rehabilitated as Manor Barns workshops.

In the 1890s gentlemen played golf on a nine hole course laid out over three meadows at Page's Lodge. Joseph Page died on Boxing Day 1901 and the tenancy of the farm passed to his son George, who did not sympathise with mixing farming and golfing. A disagreement caused cessation of golf at Stanton until 1906. Then, so that play could be resumed at the farm, the Stanton on the Wolds Golf Club was reconstituted with landlord Major Robertson strategically elected as its President. The old gig house was refurbished as a locker room and Mrs Page agreed to supply teas. A full-time greenkeeper was appointed in 1910 and the following year a horse-drawn mower was purchased. To protect the turf the horse was fitted with leather boots. Cattle and sheep wandered on the course so a gate on the road leading to the farm from Stanton Lane had to be kept closed. In the 1920s golfers came by train to Plumtree Station, where they were met by Mr Wright with his horse and brake. On their arrival at the entrance, the young Goddard

The Old Manor Farmhouse, converted from the former moated Manor House. '... it was very damp round the house.' Photograph reproduced by courtesy of Dorothy Bryans.

sisters, Marjorie and Lois, who lived opposite, would be given a penny for opening and closing the gate. In 1926 William Wallis became the professional. His shop was an old horse-drawn tram body purchased from Nottingham Corporation for £1. Following Major Robertson's death in 1926 and the sale of the farm, the Golf Club purchased about 200 acres excluding the frontage to Stanton Lane. Under the leadership of Harold Hilton and his brother-in-law Ernest Gray, the club was reconstituted as a company and a new 18 hole golf course was built on which play started in September 1928. H.G. (Peter) Gray, Ernest's son, has been the club's joint Secretary and Treasurer since 1953, when he settled in Golf Course Road.

The other farm in the village at the turn of the century was Brown's Farm, occupied by the family which gave Browns Lane its name. Their farm was 264 acres and like the Pages they had servants who lived-in. Later the farm was known as Stanton Farm and is now called Laurel Farm. Villagers lived in cottages between the rectory and the manor and also on the Waste along Stanton Lane. The Edward VII postbox was built into the wall of a cottage and there was another cottage on the lane opposite. A pair of semi-detached cottages were occupied by the Kemp family, who ran a small general shop. The present Rose Cottage replaced a small thatched cottage. The Goddard sisters lived in the front one of a pair of semi-detached cottages built end-on to the lane by the footpath. There were then fields on both sides of the lane up to the corner with Willow Brook. It was known as Harwoods Corner after the Harwoods who built Harwood House, now called The Gables, at the end of the nineteenth century. R.H. Adams owned Hill Crest, built shortly afterwards next door on Willow Brook, and also owned the surrounding fields. Very old apple trees in the back gardens of houses on this part of Stanton Lane are the remains of an orchard planted there.

Another small thatched cottage on the Waste at the beginning of Thurlby Lane belonged to the Hatherley family. Joseph Hatherley, who was a farmworker, and his wife Phoebe Hodgett from Keyworth had fourteen children. The family was badly hit by the First World War. The names of two sons who were killed, together with Thomas Kemp, are on the war memorial in the churchyard. A third son was crippled for life. A widowed daughter, Phoebe Gisborne, returned to live in the family home and it became known as Phoebe's Cottage until it was pulled down after her death.

Major Robertson's death presaged change to the old order of village life in Stanton, whose population had remained virtually unchanged since the beginning of the century. The nephew who inherited the estate decided to sell all of it. It was bought by a speculator, Mr T.P. Towle of Loughborough. He sold off Stanton Odd Houses to their sitting tenants. He also sold parcels of land for building plots on Stanton Lane, Browns Lane and Melton Road. Tenant farmers did not buy their farms and Mr Towle became their landlord. The sitting tenants at the Odd Houses included William Exton, who was the link-man on the road, at Ivy Cottage. Mr Simpson at the Post House, where there is another Edward VII postbox, was a gamekeeper on the estate and his wife was the local midwife. Their daughter later kept a small shop selling postage stamps and home-made ice cream. The Pearce family who lived in the adjoining cottage were also estate workers.

Some of the parcels of land on Melton Road and Browns Lane were sold to speculative builders who erected bungalows on them while other pieces of land were sold individually. These sales caused an influx of newcomers to the village, many of whom commuted to work in Nottingham. The Gott family had a shoe repair business in Turney Street, Nottingham. Others started their own businesses in Stanton. Mr Lowe opened a lock-up garage at the corner of Browns Lane and Melton Road. Tom Brown was a bookmaker, while his wife ran an enterprise, charging 1s 0d for afternoon tea and a game of tennis on the court at the back of their bungalow.

Increases in housing created a problem of mains water supply. In order to satisfy demand, Nottingham City Corporation, which was the water authority, erected a water tower on Browns Lane in 1932. Water was pumped up from Plumtree and was then gravity fed to houses in Stanton and Keyworth. When the source of the water supply was changed from a borehole to the Derwent reservoirs, the Severn Trent pumping station made the tower redundant and it was removed in 1985.

The 1930s were the time of pioneering experiments by Captain Athelstan Popkess, the Chief Constable of Nottingham City Police, in the use of radios in police cars. The first aerial in Stanton was in the garden of Harwood House but was removed when the Wireless Station was built on land on Browns Lane bought by Nottingham City Council. The position is the highest point in south Nottinghamshire and transmissions were made throughout the East

94

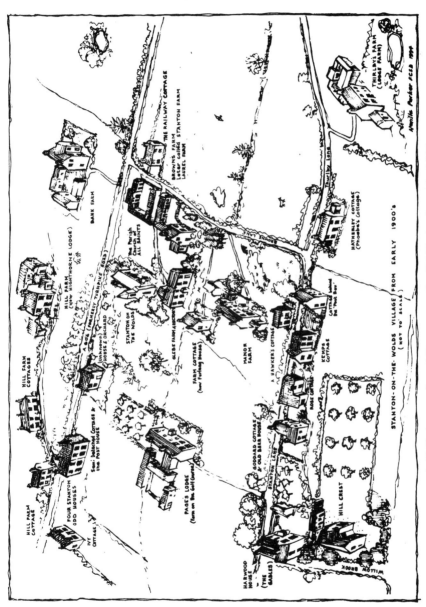

Artist's impression of Stanton on the Wolds in the early 1900s.

95

Midlands. Harold Old, who was the Regional Wireless Engineer and lived on the site, received the MBE for his pioneering services. Former employees, Albert Grice and Peter Sturt, still live there. Radio transmission from Stanton ceased in 1950 with the introduction of VHF. A Home Office workshop established on the site in 1945 continued in operation.

Guarding the Wireless Station was a duty of the Leicestershire regiment billeted locally during the Second World War. The soldiers used the forecourt of the Blue Star Garage as their parade ground. Four Stanton men served in the Home Guard: Peter Gray, Arthur Morley, Mr Wilson (the air-raid warden) and Mr Gott (the fire-picket). Mr Gott had no uniform apart from an arm-band and rode around on his bicycle looking for incendiary bombs, wearing an old saucepan on his head as a makeshift helmet. In September 1939, children from the Meadows in Nottingham were delivered to the Golf Club to be distributed to households by Albert Thraves, the billeting officer. The common room at the club house was commandeered as a schoolroom. Later, prisoners of war helped grow extra food on the farms. One worked for Mr Blount at Bank Farm and also helped the Gotts in their garden. Another worked at Manor Farm and others helped the Charlesworths at Stanton Lodge to harvest sugar beet.

After the war, plots of land were sold for building on Stanton Lane and more people came to live in the village. With the need for increased food production, more smallholding businesses were started particularly on Melton Road. In 1947, the Moores bought about five acres with a greenhouse and tractor. As building materials were scarce they were not allowed a building licence until after 1950, so they lived in a caravan. They grew vegetables as dictated by the government and kept poultry and pigs. They sold greenhouse tomatoes from a wooden hut. Today, Moores Nurseries are a busy garden centre. Also in 1947, ten acres of land were bought on Browns Lane. A plant nursery established there has developed into a nationwide wholesale business, Wolds Nurseries Limited. Iresons kept a poultry farm by the corner of Stanton Lane and Browns Lane and the Hull family ran Hillcrest Piggeries on Melton Road. Both these businesses have ceased and the pig-farm buildings are used as factory units. Bradshaws bought the milk business from Mr Wilcox of Firs Farm, Nicker Hill and initially carried the milk in churns to be measured out into customers' own jugs. Then, in the early 1950s, they built a dairy on Melton Road and installed an automated bottling plant. The dairy was recently sold to Northern Dairies, who use it for storage. In 1965 Mr Lowe sold the Blue Star Garage to National Benzole, who later sold it to Shell. It was closed down between 1980 and 1983, when Philip Hollingsworth bought it and opened the Wolds Service Station as a petrol station and shop. It is the only shop in Stanton now.

Gradually over the 50 years after Major Robertson died until the final break-up of the estate in 1977 with the sale of Laurel Farm and the old Manor Farm buildings, the tenant farmers with their mixed dairy and arable farms gave way to owner-occupier farmers. Agricultural economics have led them to diversify and contract out their land. Dairy farming has ceased in Stanton.

96

The silver medal of office of the Parish Council

Colin and Brian Hinchley at Hill Farm, which includes much of the land of the old Bank Farm, are the only farmers and agricultural contractors living in Stanton today. The Brooks run a livestock transport business at Bank Farm, which now has just 15 acres. The Kirk family bought Stanton Lodge and converted the farm buildings into Charleswold Court Nursing Home.

The last 100 years in Stanton have seen an insignificant estate village of half a dozen farms struggling to make a living on the difficult land grow into a prosperous modern community. At the last count there were 440 people living in the parish, mostly in houses built round three sides of a well tended golf course. The Queen's Silver Jubilee in 1977 was commemorated by the design and presentation of a silver medal of office by the retiring chairman of the Parish Council, Roy Butler. It depicts All Saints Church, whose unique form is a symbol of Stanton on the Wolds. The silver was provided mainly from Albert Grice's watch. Although with its modern houses Stanton serves as a dormitory village to Nottingham, much of the old village at its heart around the church and manor is still there. The Parish Council, which was created shortly after the Second World War, is concerned to conserve the past sympathetically whilst enabling imaginative future development. Would the creation of some kind of village centre provide a fitting legacy for the next generation?

97

Chapter 12

The Growth of Keyworth in the Twentieth Century

The preceding chapters have told a tale of change affecting different aspects of Keyworth life since the formation of the Parish Council in December 1894. Perhaps the most striking change of all has been the tenfold increase in population and seventeenfold increase in the number of dwellings over the past 100 years. This is dramatically expressed in the transformation of the map of Keyworth, as a comparison of Figures 6 and 7 illustrates. In the former, most of the built-up area is still concentrated along Town Street (now Main Street) and Selby Lane ('Upper Town' of Chapter 1) and Nottingham Road ('Lower Town'). Nearly all the parish land north of Bunny and Selby Lane is still shown as farmers' fields. In the latter, these same fields are almost entirely built over, while Upper and Lower Towns (no longer so called) are relatively minor elements in what has become an urbanised landscape extending for over a mile from both north to south and east to west.

In charting the developments that have brought about this transformation, a useful starting point is Figure 5, a graph showing population change in Keyworth from the first census in 1801 to the most recent in 1991, the second half of which covers the period here under review. From it we can divide Keyworth's population history during this century into four stages:

i)   from 1901 to 1921 — a period of stagnation;

ii)   from 1921 to 1951 — when there was slow but steady growth, with a 60% increase over the 30 years;

iii)   from 1951 to 1971 — when the population doubled itself in each decade, from 1330 in 1951 to 2652 in 1961 to 5754 in 1971;

iv)   from 1971 to 1991 — a return to the stagnation of the early decades of the century and even to population decline last experienced in the 1880s, coupled with a boundary change which increased the parish population by a third overnight.

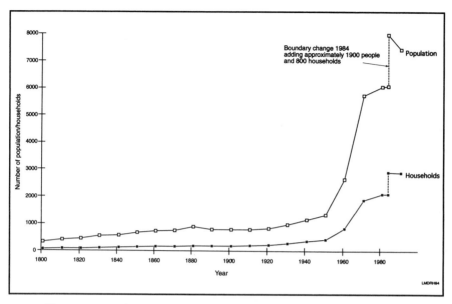

Figure 5: Population and household change in Keyworth, 1801–1991

1901 to 1921

The early years of this century, like the final decades of the last, witnessed little growth in Keyworth's population, which, in view of the high birth rates of the time probably meant continued outward migration (already commented upon for the 1880s and 1890s in Chapter 1). Framework knitting, which had sustained Keyworth's growth through most of the nineteenth century, was now in decline and no new industry had settled in the village to replace it. The railway through Plumtree, opened in 1879, offered the possibility of commuting to Nottingham. This was taken up by some, especially during the First World War when the sale of season tickets at Plumtree Station more than doubled. But more seem to have left Keyworth altogether; perhaps the walk to the station was too far and often too muddy for most.

Nevertheless, some building did take place in Keyworth, particularly between 1912 and 1916, along what is now Dale Road, the nearest part of the parish to the station via the old footpath through Plumtree Park called Sandholes. Here eight pairs of semis and a detached villa were erected. Altogether, while the population of Keyworth increased by only 6% between 1901 and 1921, the number of households (which closely approximated the number of dwellings) increased by 28%, indicating a steep drop in household size and presumably in the amount of overcrowding.

Meanwhile in neighbouring Normanton there was more substantial development, notably in Plumtree Park but also north of Debdale and Normanton Lanes. all within a few minutes' walk of the station. This formed

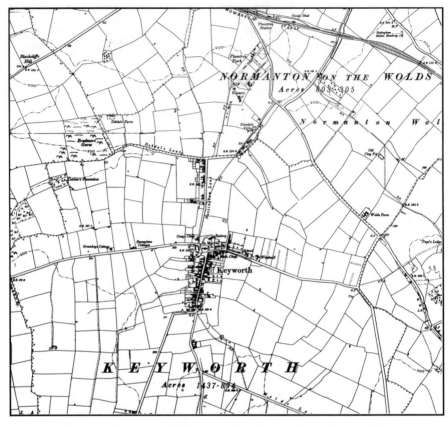

Figure 6: Keyworth 1900, from OS 6" map, 2nd edition, 1900.

the nucleus for later building which led, in 1984, to a boundary change whereby the whole of Normanton parish south of the railway line became part of Keyworth.

1921 to 1951

Population trends of the previous decades were reversed: birth rates and natural increase fell, but Keyworth's population grew, implying net *inward* migration.

The inter-war era was one of huge population movement throughout Britain. Improvements in public transport enabled millions to leave congested and polluted Victorian cities for more spacious and cleaner suburbs and rural areas beyond, and still go back each day to their place of work. The first regular motor bus service from Keyworth to Nottingham was in-

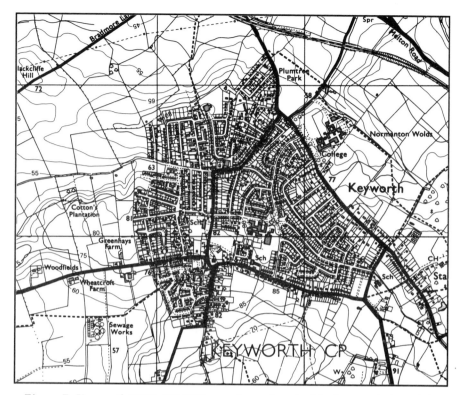

Figure 7: Keyworth 1989, OS 2½" map (reproduced with the permission of the Ordnance Survey).

troduced shortly after the First World War (see Chapter 9) and with it commuting began to play the role in the village's twentieth-century growth that framework knitting had in the nineteenth century. The number of people leaving Keyworth in search of work was, for the first time, exceeded by those working elsewhere who entered the village in search of a better place to live.

At the same time, reduction in household size continued, so that while population increased by 60% between 1921 and 1951, the number of households nearly doubled.

The new houses were not built to any overall plan. Proximity to the station was no longer a significant advantage, but access to existing roads and proximity to bus routes were. So was access to water, electricity, gas and sewerage mains when they were installed in the late 1920s and the early 1930s. As a result, the new housing took the form of ribbon development along a ring of roads comprising Nottingham Road, Normanton Lane, Nicker Hill, Willow Brook and Selby Lane, creating a mis-shapen 'doughnut' configuration with a large hole of rural land in the middle. The hole itself was

101

penetrated by three short, unmade roads and associated housing: High View Avenue (still unmade) and what are now part of Mount Pleasant ('The Twelve Apostles') and Ashley Road.

Outside the 'doughnut', three other developments occurred:

i)   the beginning of the Council Estate, along Bunny Lane, Park Avenue and Charnwood Avenue;

ii)   the laying out of Thelda Avenue parallel to Dale Road;

iii)   more building in the part of Normanton that is now in Keyworth, forming three clusters: Plumtree Park; Rose Grove and Villa Road; and the four roads leading north off Debdale Lane (Highfield and Highbury Roads, Delville and Rancliffe Avenues).

The net result of all this development was a rather untidy sprawl of housing with large intervening gaps which represented long walks between its scattered parts. The old village, where most of the services were concentrated, was at one extremity — not the most convenient arrangement for those occupying the new housing.

This kind of sporadic, low-density development was also encroaching rapidly onto rural land, not just in Keyworth but throughout much of Britain, leading to moves to contain its further spread by planning for more compact settlements in the future. The impact of these moves in Keyworth's further development was profound, as the next section demonstrates.

1951 to 1971

The pressure on rural land surrounding large cities built up after the Second World War. Bomb damage and slum clearance, followed by redevelopment at much lower housing densities than had previously been the norm, led to a need for 'overspill' estates. Added to this was the growing number who wanted to live in suburban or rural environments and, perhaps the most important factor of all, the growing ease with which people could commute as more became car owners. Modern Keyworth is, in a sense, a product of the internal combustion engine.

By now, however, the Town and Country Planning Act of 1947 had given local authorities the power to regulate where development could take place. The spread of large cities was to be contained by 'Green Belts': in the case of Nottingham, a girdle four to six miles wide stretching from the edge of the conurbation to just short of, for instance, Bingham, Kinoulton, Widmerpool, Wysall and East Leake. Demand for new housing was to be met either beyond the Green Belt, or concentrated in a few 'White Envelopes' within it — strictly defined areas where Green Belt controls were waived. One of these White Envelopes was 'Keyworth Village', which included parts of Normanton and Stanton but excluded most of Keyworth parish south of Bunny and Selby Lanes. The substantial area so designated allowed for a target population of some 8000 — a fourfold increase on the population of Keyworth and adjoining parts of Normanton and Stanton in 1951. For most of the fifties and sixties successive parts of the village were turned into huge building sites as green fields disappeared.

The Local Authority, through its Planning Department, not only regulated the general location of new development but also its detailed layout. A common principle, and certainly one that applied in Keyworth, was 'infilling', turning the sporadic clusters and ribbons of housing that had appeared particularly between the Wars into a compact settlement, thereby minimising encroachment onto 'unspoiled' rural land. The infilling had five main elements:

i)   the filling in of the hole in the doughnut with moderately priced private housing — the Wolds Drive by far the largest component;

ii)   filling the gaps in the doughnut's periphery, mainly with more expensive custom-built houses along Nicker Hill and Selby Lane;

iii)   filling in with private houses between the earlier developments in those parts of Normanton parish which were to be incorporated by a boundary change within Keyworth in 1984;

iv)   the extension northwards of the Council Estate until it occupied nearly all the area between Bunny and Debdale Lanes: today, many of these houses are privately owned;

v)   filling in the wedge of open country in the angle between the Old Village and the Council Estate: the Costain Estate.

Unlike previous decades in this century and last, and contrary to national trends, this period did not see a decline in household size. The explanation appears to be the large number of young families who moved into the new estates. Coinciding as it did with a national post-war 'bulge' in birth rates, this meant there was a disproportionate number of households with two or more children. Not that all newcomers were in large families: the considerable number of new bungalows, the smaller number of flats and the town houses on Main Street and Brook View Drive were generally occupied by older people whose families had already grown up and left home.

The rapid rise in the number of children in the village also meant a corresponding rise in demand for school places, leading to four new schools being built between 1962 and 1974 (see Chapter 4 for further details). Later, when the children had grown up and left home, and when birth rates nationally were declining anyway, there was an equally sharp fall in demand for school places. Despite the closure of the old Selby Lane School, there is now spare capacity in the new schools which only 20 years ago were bursting at the seams.

Another effect of the abrupt rise in population, and of young people in particular, was an increase in demand for open space. The Recreation Ground off Nottingham Road and the playing fields adjoining the new schools were together inadequate to meet needs and the Local Authority acquired land off Platt Lane in the late seventies to provide sporting facilities for private clubs (see Chapter 6) and also for South Wolds School — hardly an ideal solution from the school's point of view, requiring as it does a 20-minute walk each way between school and field.

Two other developments during this period should be mentioned: the opening of Cotgrave Colliery and Mary Ward College of Education. The colliery started production in 1964 but construction work began in 1957. Although most of the workforce was to be housed in Cotgrave itself, the Coal Board leased houses for miners from the Local Authority (Bingham RDC at the time) in Keyworth and other nearby villages, ferrying them to and from the mine by bus. Today the mine is closed, but commuting by bus continues, though in the reverse direction: over 120 of the 530 pupils who commute from outside Keyworth to South Wolds School come from Cotgrave.

Mary Ward College of Education was opened in what was then Normanton but is now Keyworth in 1968. It occupied Green Belt land (i.e. land outside the 'White Envelope' of Keyworth Village), illustrating the fact that such land is not sacrosanct from any form of development. Its life, however, was even shorter than that of the colliery: falling birth rates nationally meant reduced demand for teachers, and Mary Ward was one of the first colleges in the country to close in 1977. By then, the British Geological Survey was already installed and was beginning on a programme of adaptation and expansion so that today it is by far the largest employer in Keyworth, with over 500 on its staff, three-quarters of whom commute into the village.

1971 to 1991 and beyond

By 1971, nearly all the land in the Keyworth 'White Envelope' was either built upon, or allocated with building under way. The meteoric growth of the past 20 years was coming to an end. Attempts by developers to obtain permission to build south of Selby Lane, west of Rancliffe Avenue and west of Brook View Drive — i.e. on Green Belt land — were fiercely resisted by local people and turned down by the Local Authority.

The number of households increased by 12% between 1971 and 1981, mainly due to the completion of the Costain and Crossdale Estates and the northern part of the Council Estate. By the 1980s and 1990s, with very little land left to build on, household numbers hardly increased at all in the village. What building activity there was mostly took place on land where old buildings had first been demolished, such as the old people's complexes on the sites of a former cinema, the Selby Lane School and Wood Leigh House respectively; or the renovation of old farm buildings on Main Street to become up-market dwellings. The most significant exception was the building of Barnett Court, occupying former allotments off Nottingham Road, but this consists of only 13 houses.

Meanwhile the young families who moved into Keyworth in the 1950s and 1960s have aged; children have grown up and left home, so that households of four or five are often down to two today — the elderly parents. As a result, household size has fallen sharply from an average 3.08 in 1971 to 2.58 in 1991 — a drop of 16%. With little increase in the number of households it is not surprising, therefore, that the population of the village has begun to decline. For, although the population of Keyworth parish rose by nearly 1200 in the 1980s, it acquired some 2000 new residents from Normanton as a result of the 1984 boundary change, so there was a net loss to the village of around 800 or 10% of its 1981 population — proportionally similar to the fall a hundred years ago, in the 1880s.

The century of change which saw much spectacular growth and brought the transformation of Keyworth's map noted at the start of this chapter has, therefore, ended, as it began, with population decline. What of the future?

We have seen that Keyworth's 'White Envelope' is already full. Further expansion of the built-up area would be at the expense of the Green Belt, which would only be justified under pressure from a burgeoning population wishing to move to the semi-rural environment that places like Keyworth offer. Rising living standards may produce such pressure, but this must be set against the predicted decline in Britain's population over the next few decades as birth rates have fallen below replacement level. The erratic fluctuations in Keyworth's population over the past 100 years should make us wary of forecasting, but it seems that, on balance, the pressures will not be sufficient to push back the Green Belt around Keyworth, and that population numbers will settle down at about 7500 for the first quarter of the twenty-first century.

Postscript

**'Modern Keyworth is, in a sense, a product of
the internal combustion engine'**
(Chapter 12, above)

Without doubt the increasing availability of the motor car has been one of the most important developments to have occurred during this century. It has permitted a wider dispersion of the population, curtailing the growth of towns which, however, have remained by far the most important sources of employment. While the car has had a liberating effect, has made places and people accessible as never before, it has at the same time eroded social cohesion. No longer is it necessary to seek recreation or entertainment within the local community. To a considerable degree individual social needs have been met in the workplace. But where this has not sufficed, the motor car has reduced the role of the village in providing for them. Consequently the village or the parish is not perceived as being so important as formerly. This could not have been forecast in 1894; perhaps it could by 1944.

It is tempting to speculate what development now at an early stage will in the future shape our lives so significantly as the motor car. A fashionable guess is that it is most likely to be electronic communication. Already technology makes it possible to undertake at home many tasks which hitherto required people to assemble in groups in one location. Nowhere could this be more significant than in the realm of local government. Not only could many local government employees work from home, but also the whole apparatus could be dispersed so making the organization truly local. We could see at least a partial return to the pre-industrial era with major beneficial consequences. As the social dimension of office work disappears is it not possible, indeed probable, that it will be replaced by improved social interchange within the neighbourhood, parish or village? The social cohesion of the past, undermined by the motor car, might yet return along the Information Highway.